G000066103

Freney
The Robber

Michael Holden

Freney
The Robber

The Noblest Highwayman in Ireland

MERCIER PRESS
IRISH PUBLISHER – IRISH STORY

MERCIER PRESS

Cork

www.mercierpress.ie

Trade enquiries to CMD,
55a Spruce Avenue, Stillorgan Industrial Park,
Blackrock, County Dublin

© Michael Holden, 2009

ISBN: 978 1 85635 620 6

10 9 8 7 6 5 4 3 2 1

A CIP record for this title is available from the British Library

 Mercier Press receives financial assistance from the Arts
Council/An Chomhairle Ealaíon

This book is sold subject to the condition that it shall not, by way of trade or
otherwise, be lent, resold, hired out or otherwise circulated without the publisher's
prior consent in any form of binding or cover other than that in which it is
published and without a similar condition including this condition being imposed
on the subsequent purchaser.

No part of this publication may be reproduced or transmitted in any form or by
any means, electronic or mechanical, including photocopying, recording or any
information or retrieval system, without the prior permission of the publisher in
writing.

Printed and bound in the EU.

Contents

Preface

The past is never far away and will not die. It is part and parcel of what we are, and is the source from whence we came. Tales of highwaymen, outlaws, rapparees (lawless adventurers) and tories (*toraidhe*) from centuries past have held me in rapt attention over the years. I have been fascinated by swashbuckling outlaws such as Robin Hood, Dick Turpin and Long John Silver, and impressed by the courage and recklessness of these men in the face of danger and death as they plied their trade on the highways of life. The one who interested me most was our own local highwayman, James Freney – better known today as Freney the Robber. The stories of mystery told about this man around the firesides of Ireland over two and a half centuries, have elevated him to the status of legend in local folklore. He was Kilkenny's most famous highwayman, and is often referred to as the noblest of all Irish highwaymen, owing to his tact and civility in dealing with the many victims that he accosted on the roads. On many occasions, he returned – especially to ladies – items of jewellery when those at his mercy pleaded these items were of great sentimental value. It is said he even returned some of the money he had taken when victims complained that they had not enough funds to take them to their destination. He was always very courteous to the fairer sex, and careful that no insult or injury should befall his victims at the hands of his gang. He would thank them politely for their contribution, and apologise for any inconvenience caused. On account of his polish and consideration, he was dubbed the 'Gentleman Robber', and his ranking in Kilkenny's esteem is evidenced by the plaudit, 'as bold as Freney the Robber'.

His roguery and deception as a teenager were indicators of what he would become. His weakness for alcohol and gambling led him down a path from which there was no return. But his striking at the very heart of Ireland's oppressors – plundering their secure and guarded homes, and sharing his spoils with the poor – catapulted him into the limelight and elevated him to the status of local hero and, eventually, living legend.

Freney was one of the few Irish highwaymen to survive into old age and to die in his bed, though his escaping the hangman's noose owed much to his connections with Kilkenny's landed gentry.

Having researched his exploits, I find it impossible to separate fact from fiction. Freney, they say, smoked out a wedding party at a tender age; was first past the winning post in a steeplechase by sleight of hand; robbed Mount Loftus while in the company of his master; escaped detection on one occasion by changing places with a corpse; disarmed and robbed a commanding officer in the presence of his troops; reversed the shoes on his horse in order to confuse his pursuers; duped the Redcoats by claiming he was one of them and then robbing them; threatened to blow out the brains of a man he suspected of treachery; and was forced to withdraw from an attempted raid on the mansion at Killenaule – one of his few failures.

I leave it to you the reader to decide for yourself where the truth begins and ends.

Villain or Hero?
Sinner or Saint?

Outlaw, villain, robber, rogue and ruffian – just some of the descriptions of James Freney by the landed gentry and their agents. He was a thorn in their side, a nuisance and a scourge. At a time when Ireland had entered into a fairly peaceable period, along came Freney to cause havoc and mayhem, and to disrupt the economic and business life of Counties Kilkenny and Carlow. He subjected the area to a reign of robbery, hijacking and terror, the like of which had not been seen since Cromwell. His specialities were accosting travellers on the highway, and breaking into houses by smashing windows and doors with sledgehammers and making as much noise as possible so as to intimidate the occupants into submission. His activities reached such magnitude that it took the combined force of all the major landlords in County Kilkenny to subdue and eliminate this scourge.

To the downtrodden, he was a hero and a champion. He was the only light at the end of a very dark tunnel, the last bastion of hope when their whole world came tumbling down as the notice-to-quit order was nailed to the door. He helped the unfortunate people who sought his aid in their hour of need whenever he could. He risked life and limb in order to frustrate and defy the dreaded Redcoats at evictions as they administered rough justice to those unfortunate people. But he did not always rob for honourable reasons – whenever his funds ran low, he turned to the highway to fund his gambling and carousing habits.

The penal laws were in force in Ireland at that time, and no Catholic was allowed to enter the professions or own a business. If they owned a horse that the landlord took a fancy to, they would have to relinquish it to him for the miserly sum of four pounds. Taxes were levied on the number of windows and floors in their homes, and the few paltry acres they struggled to survive on were weighed down by rents and tithes. Worst of all, the practice of their religion was completely suppressed. This was the Ireland that James Freney was born into, and opinions about the notorious robber – villain or hero – depended upon which side of the social divide a person was on.

Freney was an enigma and remains so to this day. He had a dual personality; you could say there were two James Freneys, each at odds with the other. He could be a noble soul who, like Robin Hood, robbed from the rich and gave to the poor, and championed the cause of the needy and powerless; it is said that Freney never robbed or injured the poor. On the other hand, he could be a despicable rogue and often demonstrated scant respect for life or property. He was quite prepared to inflict life-threatening injury on those he suspected of betraying his loyalty or who crossed him in any way. His shrivelled eye and pockmarked face – the result of contracting smallpox at twenty-seven years of age – gave him the appearance of a desperado, and he could instill a deadly fear in those he accosted on the highway. He was prepared to rob at random, and his need for money would override any consideration for friend or foe. His utter abhorrence of the representatives of the Crown and his defiance of the law, eventually led him to the foot of the gallows.

It was the pressure of creditors and the need for money that forced Freney to embark on his life of crime. The powers-that-be and their colonial masters were his primary targets as he held them responsible for his substantial financial losses and his family's destitution after he was forced to close their public house in Waterford. 'Rob only those who are worth robbing' was his motto. He possessed a number of advantages – more so than the average criminal of his day. He was a first-class marksman, and possessed an extraordinarily cunning criminal mind. He was capable of reckless courage and took incalculable risks. He was bilingual – a crucial asset that enabled him to communicate with his associates in Irish, and ensured the authorities were kept unaware of his plans.

Freney's criminal career stretched over five years from 1744 to 1749. In this short period, he packed in some of the most courageous and audacious adventures ever to occur in Kilkenny and adjoining counties, sometimes alone and sometimes with the help of cronies. His notoriety was such that the folklore and myth that attached itself to his name has survived for over two hundred and fifty years, and there is hardly a townland in south Kilkenny that does not boast of some connection with this famous highwayman. Poems and songs were written about him, and that prolific songwriter, Percy French, wrote a comic opera – *Knight of the Road* – based on the bold Captain's adventures (he was often nicknamed Captain Freney).

Freney left a record of his exploits in the form of an autobiography, but his account confines itself to the five years in which he was involved in a life of crime. He omits to record or make any reference to the numerous occasions when he shared his ill-gotten gains with those less fortunate than himself, but local folklore reminds us of the many times when some poor unfortunate tenant faced with eviction went to Freney seeking his help, and how he was rarely found wanting. His vindictive streak would surface and assistance would be refused, however, if he recalled some misdemeanour from the past involving the individual now in need of help.

Some of the requests for assistance were at very short notice, and if Freney was inclined to help, he might have no time to summon his accomplices. Instead, he would run the risk alone, save for the company of his trusted mare, Beefsteaks, and a pair of flintlocks – sometimes even less, when he would improvise with cabbage stalks. He was prepared to risk life and limb as he accosted overzealous rent collectors and their portly protectors in an effort to prise from them the blood money collected from the wretched tenants.

He was a loveable rogue and his actions were not always

prompted by greed and revenge. He got great satisfaction from observing some of these high-and-mighty people cower when confronted with his menacing blunderbuss. He built up a network of intelligence throughout Kilkenny and Carlow, employing those whom he had befriended in their hour of need and people like himself who lived on the fringes of society. It is said that he was gifted with outstanding leadership qualities, and could plan and execute any manoeuvre with military precision – something that enabled him to outwit those who pursued him in the name of law and order. Had his undoubted courage and talents been put to work in the cause of nationalism, he would more than likely occupy a place in history on a par with Michael O'Dwyer or Patrick Sarsfield. Alas, that was not to be.

Freney was a product of his time – compelled to embark on a life of highway robbery and grand larceny in an effort to free himself from the miserable existence forced upon him and his kind by their colonial masters. Trickery and roguery were the order of the day, yet he was an honourable rogue who showed civility to women and who had compassion for most of his fellow men. Death clearly held no fear for him – the courage and determination he displayed when engaged in some of his exploits give a strong indication of this.

In common with most criminals, his luck eventually ran out. Members of his gang betrayed him in order to save their own necks. Left with only one option for survival, he put into practice the old proverb, 'Do unto others as they do unto you', and managed to avoid the walk to the gallows. When granting Freney a pardon, an overriding consideration for the authorities was the fact – a most surprising fact – that no record or report existed of him having ever taken a human life. There were many reports of soldiers being severely wounded during a shoot-out with the bold Captain, but – fortunately for him – none ever succumbed to their injuries. However, only the jamming of his pistol on a number of occasions prevented him from entering the history books as a murderer and ending his life dangling from a rope. Thus, unusual among highwaymen, Freney was to die of old age in his bed.

Early Life in Ballyduff

In the verdant and tranquil countryside of south Kilkenny, lying in the ancient diocese of Ossory, surrounded and dissected by the three sister rivers, nestles the beautiful village of Inistioge. Near here, in the year 1719 or thereabouts, was born a child whose name will live on in the history of this region as long as the land of saints and scholars remains on the map. This man was James Freney – now known to us as Freney the Robber or Bold Captain Freney, the notorious highwayman.

James Freney's father, John, was employed on the Robbins estate at Ballyduff near Inistioge. As time passed, he acquired knowledge of horticulture, and subsequently was promoted from general labourer to head gardener. John's dependability and scrupulous approach to his work eventually saw him appointed head steward on the estate. James Freney's mother, Alice Phelan, also worked for the Robbins, as a parlour maid, and after walking out with John for some time, the two were married. Alice continued to work on the estate, but later had to leave the Robbins' service and go to her father's house nearby for her confinement, prior to the birth of a son who was christened James.

It was at this time that John Freney was promoted to the position of head steward. As he was now a married man with responsibilities, he was allocated a house on the Robbins estate, and took up residence with his wife and son. Given John's prestigious position on the estate, the lifestyle of the Freney family must have been far removed from the subsistence existence of the average tenant. It was here, in the surrounds of the Ballyduff estate on the banks of the silvery Nore, that young James spent his childhood. He was doted on by old Mrs Robbins, the matriarch of the Robbins clan. She looked on him as one of her own, as she had constant contact with him as he accompanied his father about the courtyard and estate while he attended to his duties.

Old Mr Robbins died in the early 1720s and was succeeded by his son George, who continued to employ John Freney as head steward, thus enabling young James' protected lifestyle to continue. As a child, his quick wit, fierce curiosity, gift of conversation, polite nature and his love of animals endeared him to all who came in contact with him. He established himself as a firm favourite with the new generation at Ballyduff House.

Young James' schooling commenced in Inistioge and, according to his autobiography, he attended school for seven years. Old Mrs Robbins had such regard for the young boy that she employed a private tutor to instruct him in the proper manner of the day, at her own expense, in her home in Ballyduff. She installed him in the kitchen as a pantry boy so as he would be near to her at. His duties there would have been menial: collecting tableware, washing kitchen crockery and cutlery, polishing boots and shoes, and fetching coal for the fires. He was at old Mrs Robbins' beck and call at all times. He would have been very familiar with many of the aristocratic and influential people who came to Ballyduff to visit, and would have mingled freely among them while he attended to his duties and saw to their needs.

He had the freedom of the house and soon developed a taste for the finer things in life, such as good food and fine wine, and it is not beyond the realms of possibility that he indulged himself in the many exotic substances of the day, such as snuff and tobacco. As he entered his teens, James enjoyed the pleasure of the rural pursuits of the day. He developed a taste for gambling and drinking, and was soon to be found in all the local inns, alehouses and shebeens in and around Inistioge, Thomastown and Graiguenamanagh. He was addicted to horse racing, and attended all the local sporting events, mostly organised by the Big Houses for the entertainment of their employees and tenants. Due to the generosity of his benefactors, the Robbins family, he had at his disposal one of the finest horses in the district, and wagered heavily on his chances of success. He was always willing and ready to throw down the gauntlet to anyone who boasted that their abilities in the saddle were superior to his. It is likely that those early successes caused him to develop an air of invincibility that influenced his later choice of lifestyle, and which eventually would set him on a collision course with the law. His father had tried in vain to put correction on him, but to no avail as old Mrs Robbins was always on hand to intercede for the wayward James. He continued on this merry-go-round of races, dances, cockfights, dogfights, hurling matches and every kind of diversion that came his way. If anybody was looking for young James, he was usually found in the darkest corner of an alehouse or shebeen and involved in a game of cards, from which he took great satisfaction when relieving his cronies of the meagre few shillings they could ill afford to lose. His keen eye and sharp intellect enabled him to take full advantage of any opportunity that came his way. He attended local barn dances, and is said to have been a first-class dancer – very light of foot. He had a very good ear for music, and was an accomplished player on the reed whistle. By this time, he had acquired an eye for the girls, and was considered a good catch on account of his standing in the Robbins' household.

James' father became worried about the direction his son was taking, and suggested to Mrs Robbins that he would be better employed as an apprentice to some trade or other. She strongly objected, saying that he was now indispensable to her. But in order to put his mind at ease, she apprenticed young James to the estate's malt maker. This may be where he got the idea of going into the liquor business when – later – he tried his luck in the world of enterprise. But for now, the new arrangement did nothing to alter his ways. He was absent more often than not, as he continued to pursue his foolhardy ways. He developed a reputation as a hard-drinking sporting hero, and his many friends and cronies held him in very high regard. They found him to be a person in whom they could confide, and from whom they could seek help when in need of financial assistance for weddings, funerals or dowries. James was therefore able to supplement his income through a money-lending operation at a time when banks were few and far between.

As old Mrs Robbins was at this time in the twilight of her years, she was in no position to keep any measure of control over her young charge, and James was his own master. He was now very familiar with every nook and cranny of Counties Kilkenny, Carlow, Waterford and Wexford, and was acquainted with every dog and devil from Castlecomer to New Ross. All-night card playing, drinking and carousing were the order of the day, and his finances were often in a sorry state. However, his ability in the saddle and the quality of the horses available to him usually ensured the cash flow necessary for his precarious lifestyle.

By this time, James was a major attraction at the annual sports competitions held by local landlords: hurling and football matches, athletics meetings and equestrian events. To be successful at any of these was a significant achievement. If an individual was considered good enough by a landlord, he might issue a challenge to a neighbouring estate, and the individual would be pitted in combat for the glory and honour of His Lordship. A hefty wager was usually riding on the outcome, so success was important in order to stay on the right side of the landlord. Young Freney often found himself in this situation, and very seldom disappointed the Robbins family. His success in the saddle convinced the Robbins family to allow him to represent them in other events, including the best-shot competition. James was an excellent shot, and with the benefit of long hours of practice and first-rate weaponry supplied by the estate, he became one the best marksmen in the area – something that would stand him in good stead when he later embarked on his career of plundering and ransacking the households of the gentry.

The Robbins family was immensely proud of James Freney's achievements, and would not entertain anyone disapproving of him. He had by this time attained the stature of superhero, and revelled in the acclaim that was heaped upon him. His drinking, gambling and carousing continued apace until the death of his benefactor – old Mrs Robbins – in 1742, at which time he decided to change the course of his life.

Smoked Out at the Wedding

This story provides a fine example of how James Freney's leadership qualities were evident in his early teenage years. A wedding celebration was in full swing at the home of one of his father's neighbours in Ballyduff. All the family's relations and friends were invited to join in the festivities. A night of music, song and dance was being enjoyed by all when a group of young frolickers barged their way into the kitchen and proceeded to join in the merriment. This band of delinquents were led by young James Freney, who had just entered his teenage years and who held, even at this tender age, an ever-increasing influence over the rest of his young companions. The bride's father told them they were too young to be there, and asked them to leave, saying that it was long past their bedtime. Young Freney verbally abused him, telling him that he was an old stick-in-the-mud and a killjoy who was more than lucky to be getting his ugly daughter off his hands. The father – not in any mood to tolerate such abuse – made a dive at the young whelp with a view to evicting him from the house. The agile youngster sidestepped his assailant and tripped him as he lunged past, sending him crashing into the dresser. With the man now in a heap on the clay floor, Freney and his companions exited the kitchen in double-quick time. On his way out, Freney grabbed the whisk broom and a cloak from behind the kitchen door and pulled it out after him. He put the handle of the broom through the latch, catching it against both jams so as to secure the door, thus ensuring it could not be opened from inside. He plunged the cloak into a barrel of water – saturating it – and then threw it up onto the thatched roof. He climbed up on a cart parked alongside the gable, and worked his way up onto the roof and over to the chimney. Freney draped the saturated cloak across the opening to the chimney, and then scampered down the thatch and onto the ground. In a matter of moments, the kitchen was filled with the stench of soot and smoke, clogging the lungs of the revellers and prompting a stampede to the door. The door failed to yield, and soon all those inside were coughing and choking. The bride's father had to break a window and heave one of the guests out through it so he could release the securely held broom. The merrymakers trooped out into the yard to relieve their aching lungs, swearing vengeance on the young rogue. Freney and his companions could be heard laughing heartily as they made good their retreat.

Sleight of Hand at Borris

Two years later, we find young Freney taking on the might of the equestrian and racing world when the landlord of Borris House, Mr McMurragh-Kavanagh, held a sports day on his estate for his employees and those of his adjoining neighbours. He took great pride in the fact that an employee of his had succeeded in winning the five-mile cross-country steeplechase for three-year-old horses for two years in succession. This man's ability in the saddle was so good that McMurragh-Kavanagh put up a purse of a hundred gold sovereigns by way of a challenge to anybody who would take on and beat his champion. Given the jockey's success, it was proving difficult to find an opponent to take him on. His Lordship had every confidence in him, and believed that his wager was safe and sound. The Robbins of Ballyduff estate considered it pointless to take up the challenge from their Borris neighbour, but had no objection to any of their employees taking their chances. Young Freney – only fifteen years of age at this time – rose to the challenge. When he and his cronies arrived at Borris House on the day of the race, a huge crowd had assembled on the lawn, and hefty wagers were being laid out. As they lined up at the starting post, Freney stood up in his stirrups and announced that he would wager two-to-one against any man that he would not be beaten. His bluff was called: a wager of a hundred pounds was placed, and the race began.

The race consisted of two laps over a two-and-a-half-mile course that started and finished in front of the Big House. The participants had to jump dykes, ditches and stone walls that passed through woodland and scrubland on the fringe of the estate before returning to the Big House. However, Freney had sneaked into Borris a week before the race and inspected the course. Having sized it up, an idea occurred to him that would help him take home the coveted prize. He conceived a plan to station one of his cronies – of equal size to himself and clothed in like attire – on a horse identical to his own in the wooded area of the racecourse, and to hide there until the race began. His plan was to keep ten to twelve lengths behind the leader as they entered the wood, and at a spot where the course took a sharp bend his accomplice would fall in behind the leader. Freney would drop out to await the return of the competing horses on the second lap, where he would again exchange places with his accomplice, only now on a comparatively fresh horse, and complete the race.

All went according to plan, and on the second lap Freney rejoined the race and gradually made up ground. As they came in sight of the Big House, he drew level and went on to win by a short head. McMurragh-Kavanagh suffered the indignity of seeing his champion defeated, and was obliged to part company with the prize money. He also lost a hefty wager. The man who covered Freney's challenge also had to pay up, and discovered on relinquishing his two hundred pounds that Freney's saddlebags were in fact empty. The audacity and self-confidence of the youth was such that he would not countenance defeat.

It must have been very satisfying for the youngster to come away with three hundred pounds in his saddlebag that a short while before had been empty. Wit, optimism and cunning had won the day and ensured a respectable purse for the sly young scoundrel, and must surely serve as a pointer to his later conflicts with the law.

Race Day in Thomastown

A major sports meeting comprising athletic events such as tug-of-war, sheaf pitching, weight throwing, running and horse racing was held beside the river in Thomastown every summer. The prize for the major horse event was a brand new saddle. This enticed some of the best horsemen in Kilkenny to come and try their luck. On two previous occasions Freney had come within a hair's breadth of bringing home this coveted prize. A competitor from near Kilkenny city had beaten him two years running, and this had put a dent in his growing reputation. Not surprisingly, he was eager to prove that it was bad luck and not superior horsemanship that had defeated him on those occasions.

He contrived a wicked plan to get the better of his arch rival. On the night before the race, he went to the yard in Thomastown where this man stabled his horse, and scratched two abrasions on the skin under its tummy directly in line with where the saddle girth would rest. He coated the girth with a mixture of turpentine and vinegar, knowing that when the horse heated up during the race and began to perspire, the corrosive mixture would seep into the abrasions and aggravate the animal so that it would become unmanageable.

The afternoon was bright and sunny, and a large crowd assembled for the sport. As evening approached, the competitors for the horse race were called to the starting post. All eyes were riveted on the two chief contenders as the throng pondered which of them would take home the laurels on this occasion. Freney and Beefsteaks looked an impressive sight, and hefty wagers were laid on them as well as on several of the other contestants. Freney's chief rival seemed in fine fettle and looked every inch a winner. The race got underway, and all went well until midway through the second circuit when the horse of Freney's rival let fly a backlash and careered off to one side. The jockey tried in vain to control the agitated animal and to get it back on course. It appeared to have developed a frenzied craziness and acted as if possessed by the devil. The horse then bolted – unseating his rider – and disappeared along the river bank, lashing out with its hind legs as it fled.

Freney won the race and was receiving his prize when his rival hobbled back into the enclosure, complaining that he did not know what had got into his animal and that it had never behaved like that before. Later that night, in one of the local inns, Freney boasted that it was sleight of hand that had enabled him to take home the coveted prize. It was days later when his rival discovered the reason for his horse's strange behaviour, but by then it was too late to do anything to rectify the situation. The cunning rogue had won the day, and it was said that he used

that same saddle on many of his most outlandish escapades as
he robbed and plundered the homes of the people who probably
donated it as the prize on that occasion.

Party at Ballyduff House

It was customary at Halloween for the Robbins family to entertain their friends at Ballyduff House and its pleasant surroundings. All the invited guests were treated to the usual Halloween festivities, including games, dancing and singing. They were wined and dined, and Halloween pranks were played during the evening. Young James Freney was by now a butler in the Robbins household, and on one such occasion – when supper was over and the guests were enjoying the games and pastimes laid on for their entertainment – he enquired of Mr Robbins if he would be needed again that evening. He said he was feeling unwell and wished to retire to bed. Mr Robbins told him to go rest and take good care of himself. Freney went to his room, but rather than go to bed, he slipped out the window, retrieved his musket and went straight to the home of one of the guests, a short distance away. Here, he helped himself to a selection of very fine plate and some forty sovereigns he found hidden in a silver teapot.

As he was about to leave the house, he heard voices coming from outside. Unknown to him, the servant girl had taken advantage of her master's absence to have a clandestine meeting with her lover. They were making their way back to the house after spending some time canoodling and courting in the stables. As they unlocked the door, Freney, caught unawares, had to dive for cover, and he took refuge behind some heavy curtains. The amorous pair let themselves into the house and began to kiss and smooch only feet away from where the felon was hiding. Getting carried away with their activities, they lost their balance and crashed against the curtains that were concealing Freney. He was knocked against the window, and the rattling of the plate in his bag alerted the pair to his presence. His quick thinking came to his rescue: he grabbed the curtains, and with one mighty jerk brought them tumbling down on top of the amorous couple.

Bounding to the doorway, he disappeared into the night, leaving the startled duo to untangle themselves from the curtains. He made his way back to Ballyduff with haste, knowing that the alarm would be raised immediately. He had just gained the safety of his room when the commotion started downstairs; the lovebirds had arrived to report the robbery. Consternation broke out and all the guests prepared to go home to see if they, too, had been victims of the cheeky robber. Mr Robbins went to the servants' quarters to instruct Freney to assist the guests as they departed. Finding him apparently sound asleep in his bed, he changed his mind – feeling sorry for him – and returned to aid his guests as best he could. The next morning, as Freney was serving breakfast to his master, he was informed of the occurrences of the night before, and told of the excitement he had missed. Freney replied that Mr Robbins was lucky to have been hosting a party, since he could otherwise have been a victim of the thief. Mr Robbins did not for one moment suspect that he was in the presence of the perpetrator of this daring robbery.

The Apparition

Mrs Robbins went on holiday to her childhood home in Piltown every year. She looked forward to meeting her relatives and old school friends, and was happy to leave Ballyduff to its own accord, having the greatest confidence in the younger members of the Robbins' clan to take care of themselves. This they did with relish, and as soon as she had left for Piltown, they sent word to their friends to come and join them for a few days of merriment and relaxation. Their friends duly arrived, and Freney was responsible for installing them in their respective sleeping quarters. He hated these interruptions to the usual routine of the house as it meant a lot more work for him and the staff, and curtailed their time off.

Little did he think that things could get worse, until the next day, when a distant cousin of the Robbins family arrived unannounced from England to pay them a short visit. This cousin was in the shipping trade, and whenever he came to the port of New Ross he called to see his Irish relatives. Freney – who had a very strong dislike for this gentleman owing to his authoritarian and haughty manner and his demeaning treatment of the servants – was ordered to show the visitor to his bedroom so he could refresh himself before the evening meal. As all the bedrooms in the house were occupied by the other visitors, the only one left available was the master bedroom, where Mrs Robbins slept. Here, he installed the English seafarer. This was the most elaborate bedroom in the house and contained a canopied four-poster bed surrounded by curtains that drew together midway across the end facing the doorway. Things got worse for Freney after the English visitor reprimanded him vigorously for letting his portmanteau fall as he carried it up to the bedroom. He accused him of damaging it and causing some of the contents to spill. This rebuke only increased Freney's dislike of the visitor, and his resentment of him increased by the hour.

After supper, the Robbins family and their guests adjourned to the sitting room to smoke and engage one another in idle banter. The English visitor told a story of an uncanny encounter he had as he lay in bed the night before he sailed to Ireland. He told them that as he was on the point of falling asleep, he noticed a woman dressed completely in white standing at the end of his bed. She bore a forlorn demeanour as she stared directly at him. She then faded into the gloom of the night, emitting a low, mournful sigh that caused him to break out in a clammy sweat. He told the assembled party that he hoped it was not an ill omen.

Freney overheard this tale as he came and went with decanters of wine and boxes of snuff for the merrymakers, and a preposterous scheme took shape in his mind. He was well aware that the household pet, an Irish wolfhound, had a habit of going up to the bedroom door each morning, pushing it open with his nose, and entering the room and rising up on his hind legs to look in over the end of the bed to greet Mrs Robbins. He waited until the early hours of the morning to put his plan into action. He brought in the wolfhound from its kennel, secured a white sheet around its body, fitted a white pixie-type sleeping cap over its head, and proceeded to the master bedroom. He raised the latch quietly and allowed the dog to enter the room.

True to form, the dog raised himself up on the end of the bed and poked his head in between the drawn curtains. Sensing that the mistress was not there, he began to sniff loudly at the strange scent of the seafarer. The sleeping man was jolted awake by the noise, and seeing the white form peering in at the end of his bed let out a mighty screech that awakened the whole house. The poor dog got such a fright that he bounded back down the stairs and scuttled to his kennel.

Freney was there to remove the evidence of his roguery, and rushed into the house enquiring what all the commotion was about. The rest of the household were in the Englishman's room enquiring what had befallen him and attempting to pacify him. They plied him with whiskey to try to calm him, and eventually got the story from him. He rattled and babbled on about the woman in white appearing at the end of his bed. He departed for New Ross at first light the next morning, hoping to get back to England before some terrible catastrophe befell him or his family. He firmly believed that the apparition he witnessed was a forewarning of some disaster to come. Some months later, Freney divulged to his drinking partners that it was he and not the supernatural that blighted the Englishman's visit to Ballyduff.

Sorry For Your Trouble
Mrs Joyce

A substantial merchant in the village of Inistioge, Mr Joyce – under the influence of drink – had mislaid a quart bottle of sovereigns, and organised a search of his yard and premises to locate the missing money. His servant boy located the cash in a tub of malt and dutifully returned it to his master. Word of this spread around the village, and, on hearing about it, Freney decided there would be easy pickings. That night after dark, dressed in a hooded cape, and his face camouflaged with a mixture of soot and axle grease, he made his way to the Joyce home. He knocked on the door, and Mrs Joyce enquired from within who was there. Disguising his voice, he answered that it was her sister's servant with a letter for her. She opened the door, and he burst in and demanded to know where the money was. She told him that Mr Joyce had taken it to New Ross to lodge it in the bank, as he feared it might be stolen. He paid her no heed, but a thorough search of the house failed to turn up the cash. All he found was a handful of sovereigns, a few trinkets of plate and some jewellery that she said was of great sentimental value to her. In his frustration, he took the lot with him. Next morning, news of the robbery was all over the village. When Freney was told of it, he said it was an outrage, and proceeded to call on Mrs Joyce to express his disgust at what had happened to her. He told her the country was alive with thieves, robbers and every kind of ruffian imaginable, and that law and order had broken down. He enquired of her how much she had lost, and if she had been injured in any way. She told him how lucky they had been not to suffer any injury or to lose the bottle of sovereigns. She explained to Freney how her husband had replaced the bottle in the tub of malt for safety, and how at the time the thief had called, Mr Joyce was in the malt house enjoying a quiet drink that he hoped she was not aware of. The thief, she said, seemed a dim fellow, and she hoped he would be apprehended soon. She thanked Freney for his concern, and expressed her wish that all the people in the village would be as considerate as he was. He bid her goodbye and departed, raging that he had failed in his intent the night before, but content with the knowledge that he was not under suspicion. This was one of the few times in his life when the quarry outwitted the hunter.

Mount Loftus Treasure
in Kilfane

Lord Carrick, who was one of the Ormond Butlers, held a party at his home in Ballylinch which is now known as Mount Juliet. Lots of the leading socialites of County Kilkenny attended, including Mr Robbins of Ballyduff House. Freney went along in the coach with Mr Robbins as his personal attendant. These parties began around six o'clock in the evening and continued until midnight. Those guests who lived more than five miles away would stay the night, and those who lived close at hand would return to their respective homes. The weather took a turn for the worse during the evening, with high winds and torrential rain developing. Lord Carrick insisted that all his guests stay the night. Their various entourages had to be accommodated in the servants' quarters, and their horses settled in the stables in Ballylinch. Freney – who was very familiar with the servants' quarters – secured himself a cubicle at the rear of the room that had a window overlooking a low roof. This would allow him easy access to come and go if he so wished.

Earlier, while he was mingling among the other servants, he overheard that one of the guests, John Eaton, the owner of the Mount Eaton estate (known to us today as Mount Loftus, which lies between Graiguenamanagh and Goresbridge), had a substantial amount of money, silver plate and very valuable jewellery concealed in a safe at his home. Freney decided to relieve the good gentleman of his valuable possessions while he was away from home. After retiring to bed at ten o'clock, he waited for an hour until the others were asleep, and then commenced his plan of action. He slipped out the window and acquired a horse from one of the stables. Taking a shortcut through Kilfane, Castlegarden and Raheenroche, and on to Powerstown, he was at Mount Eaton's gates in little over an hour. He was very familiar with the layout of this estate as he had visited it on several occasions with his employer. He knew of a shed at the back of the stables used by the blacksmith as a forge. He brought his horse to this shed, stripped off its flat shoes, reversed them and tacked them back on again, leaving it in readiness for a quick departure. He covered his face with a square of thick linen blackened by car grease, and made his way to the back of the house. Here, he forced a window on the ground floor and entered the drawing room. He had a good knowledge of the layout of the house from earlier visits, and made his way to the mistress' bedroom. He greeted her kindly, saying he intended her no harm but that he had fallen on hard times and was in need of a little money. She screamed to her servants for help and two of them came running. Freney locked them in the wardrobe and politely asked the lady of the house to lead the way to the safe. Having no option, she took the keys from under her pillow and led him downstairs. Under the stairs in the hallway, she opened a hidden door, and there in front of him was the largest safe he had ever seen – nearly as high as himself and some three feet in width. Opening it, he found sacks of assorted gold and silver coins, several items of gold jewellery and an amount of silver plate.

Freney returned Mrs Eaton to the bedroom and locked her in the wardrobe with the servants. Then he set about removing the treasure from the safe. He transferred the money to his saddlebags, wrapped the plate and jewellery in two sheets, took out the lot and secured them on his horse. He returned to the bedroom, released his captives from the wardrobe, thanked the mistress for her generosity, said he hoped he had not inconvenienced her too much, and bid her good night.

He set out on his return journey to Lord Carrick's by the exact same route he had come, but on approaching Kilfane Castle, he decided to hide his booty. He considered it too risky to take it too near his master's estate in Ballyduff or to Lord Carrick's in Ballylinch. He decided the best place to conceal it was on the Bushe estate in Kilfane, knowing that no one would venture in there and the chance of it being found by accident was fairly remote. As he rode through the estate in the darkness, he was on the lookout for a place to hide his loot. He came to the high wooded area known as Cnock Hill – wrongly pronounced today as Knox's Hill – at the southern side of the avenue leading to the Big House. He made out the outline of a very tall tree against the skyline and chose to bury his loot underneath its roots. He estimated his capture that night was in the region of four to five hundreds pounds – not a bad night's taking by any standard. Freney returned to Lord Carrick's, replaced the horse in its stable, reset its shoes correctly, and returned to his bed without anyone knowing he had been gone.

The sun was shining the next morning and a bright new day saw everybody looking forward to returning home. The mood changed when a horseman arrived in great haste from Mount Eaton with word of the daring robbery. It never dawned on anyone that one of the guests at Lord Carrick's had been involved, as they were all seen to go to bed the night before and were all present when called in the morning. The authorities were informed and they began an investigation immediately. They could find no evidence of anybody leaving Mount Eaton estate on horseback that night – only hoof marks leading in. This led them to believe that locals were responsible for the crime and had got away on foot.

Some weeks later – when things had quietened down – Freney returned to Kilfane to recover his prize. He was not aware that two nights after he had buried his loot, a severe storm had ravaged Kilfane, knocking down many trees including the tall one under which he chose to conceal his ill-gotten gains. He could not locate his landmark and so could not find where his hoard was hidden. All the trees in the area appeared of equal height and no tree stood out taller than the rest. He made several trips back and forth to Kilfane at night in the hope of finding his buried treasure, but to no avail.

The area he was searching was very close to the Big House, so he could not spend too much time looking around for fear of been caught and having to explain his presence there. He made several attempts to recover his prize, but it is believed he was never successful and that he had to abandon his efforts in case Henry Bushe – the owner of Kilfane – was informed of a stranger trespassing on his land.

The story is still told in Kilfane about a man who lived in the gate lodge at the entrance to Kilfane House at the end of the nineteenth century. He spent all his spare time searching and digging under trees in the hope of finding Freney's hidden treasure. To the best of local knowledge, luck was not on his side and the loot may still be lying in Cnock Hill, awaiting the day when some unsuspecting soul will let the sun shine again on John Eaton's missing gold.

Card Game at Ballylinch

On one of the occasions when Freney accompanied Mr Robbins to Lord Carrick's, he was invited to join in a game of cards by some of the employees on the estate. Many of them were addicted to gambling, but none more so than himself. He was noted for taking outlandish risks and it was the ambition of many a local card player to pit their talents against his. He never backed down from a challenge, and after playing for time, found himself having to wager his beloved mare Beefsteaks against a cabin and a pratie plot put up by a man under the influence of drink, who could ill afford to lose. Freney took up the challenge, and, true to the old saying, 'the devil's children have the devil's luck', he won the game. The beaten man, realising that he had left his wife and young family without a roof over their heads, roared that he was going to the river to drown himself. Freney grabbed him by the collar of his coat, dragged him out into the yard and forced his head into a barrel of water. He repeated this three times and waited until the man came to his senses. When he did, he began to stutter and babble about losing the bet, but Freney told him that he was suffering from hallucinations brought on by the drink, that it had affected his mind, and that he had dreamt the whole thing. He made the man swear that he would never gamble again, saying that if he did he would come back and blow his brains out. This story illustrates Freney's humanity; he was not always prepared to fleece a man for his own personal gain.

Business Venture in Waterford

Freney had been walking out with a local girl for some time, and decided to get married and settle down. By now he was in his twenties and reaching that stage when a man had to make something of himself. His patron – old Mrs Robbins – had recently died, and he knew that change was imminent.

With the dowry his wife Ann brought with her, and with the money he had himself, they went to Waterford and set up a public house. But it was not long before he found himself at odds with the authorities. The penal laws were in force at this time, and no native Irish person was allowed to enter the professional or business world without prior approval from the powers-that-be. Freney had overstepped his station in life, and was about to be made aware of this in no uncertain manner. The authorities demanded quarterage fees from him, and warned him that if he did not pay, they would apply sanctions against him in order to force him out of business. Freney felt this was very unfair and swore to defy them. Though the pressure was kept up for months he was unyielding, and an ultimatum was issued to the effect that he had to pay up or be seized upon.

Freney went to the city chambers to plead his case, but received no hearing. He was told that the law applied to all and that no man was exempt, and he was again warned that unless he paid up, his goods and chattels would be taken and his premises closed. Freney reacted by abusing the authorities, and swore that any man who dared come near his home would suffer the indignity of having his brains blown out. But after a few days during which he reflected on his dilemma, he concluded that he could not win. John Bull would see him forced out of business.

Freney closed his public house at great financial loss, and returned to Inistioge. Having installed his wife and child at her parents' house, he went to Thomastown to stay with a friend. He was a very angry, disappointed and frustrated man. He had invested all their money in setting up the venture, and now found himself at a very great loss. This was also the first time he had found himself at the receiving end of the negative side of the ascendancy class – something from which he had been sheltered while on the Robbins estate. He now became aware of the oppressive system in operation in his own country, and of how the forces of occupation were hell-bent on keeping it that way. Freney swore to have his revenge.

To the Highway

Having spent time in Thomastown without occupation, the last of his money was gone, and Freney found himself in serious trouble with his debtors. One night, as he was drowning his sorrows in a local inn, he fell into conversation with a stranger and unloaded all his tales of woe on him. The stranger told him that he knew of a way by which Freney could unburden himself of his debt and put money in his pocket. Unbeknownst to him, Freney was about to embark on the greatest adventure of his life. The stranger told him his name was Reddy, and that he was a member of the Kellymount Gang – a band of small-time robbers notorious for stealing horses, cattle and sheep from local farmers. He told Freney of an upcoming fair in the town and of the attendance there of agents of the landed gentry with large amounts of money for buying cattle. He suggested they waylay them on the highway on their way to the fair, and relieve them of their money. The mention of landed gentry was like a red rag to a bull to Freney. Their kind had dealt him a severe blow during his venture in Waterford. His anger and bitterness against them resurfaced, and he revelled in the thought of getting even.

Over the next two weeks he deliberated on the situation, and finally succumbed to the thought of easy money. Freney would become a highwayman. He and Reddy arranged to meet early on the morning of the fair, and to take up a position on the high road between Ballyhale and Thomastown, so as to accost their victims as they made their way to the fair. They blackened their faces with axle grease, and with primed blunderbusses waited for their quarry in the pre-dawn darkness. This was a new departure for the two men. Reddy had stolen cattle and sheep before, but had never robbed anybody at gunpoint. Freney had swindled and rooked many a man, but had never gone as far as robbing so brazenly with a blunderbuss on the king's highway. They must have felt a little apprehensive and nervous about risking their lives in an attempt to relieve the cattle barons of their trading funds.

Having waited in the ditch for some time, their patience growing thin, Reddy suggested they head into town. Freney declined, saying he was too well known there and the risk was too great. Reddy told Freney to suit himself before mounting his horse and heading off to Thomastown. Freney lingered, but only a few tenant farmers passed by on their way to the fair, and he was about to return home when he heard the clip-clop of a horse's hooves approaching. He stood close to the ditch, his primed blunderbuss gripped tightly in his hand as he waited nervously for the rider to come abreast of him. Stepping out on to the road, he called out, 'Stand and deliver'.

The horseman, caught by surprise, begged for mercy. 'For God's sake, don't shoot me.'

Freney demanded he hand over his money. The traveller stalled, saying that he was going to meet a friend at the fair to deliver this horse to him and would have no money until he was paid for the animal. However, the touch of cold steel against his jaw and Freney's insistence that his voice betrayed his bluff, was enough to change his mind. He was advised that if he desired to live to see his friend again, he had better hand over his money. Freney was surprised at how quickly the traveller produced his purse, and realised the effect that cold steel had on a man's nerve and how quickly it would cause him to capitulate. His victim produced a pouch and proffered it to Freney, who grabbed it. Feeling the bulk, he knew he had made a worthwhile capture. He backed away from the rider while thanking him for his cooperation, and the traveller muttered curses as he watched Freney disappear in the haze of the breaking dawn.

Once the bold robber had retreated some distance in the direction of Ballycocksouis he reined up to inspect his catch. On opening the pouch, he counted out fifty gold sovereigns. His adrenalin pumped to new heights as he gazed at his prize, and this first flush of success convinced him that he had indeed found his true calling in life. James Freney was convinced that the highway was the road to easy pickings. Little did he know then that it would also lead him to the very gates of hell.

Operating alone was not entirely practical, so Freney formed a gang. Robbing on the highway was one thing, but breaking into secure and guarded homes demanded expertise of a different kind. Unlike the thieves of today, who prefer to operate as silently as possible and without interference from the occupants, Freney and his gang made no attempt to conceal their presence. In fact, they liked to intimidate their victims by making as much noise as possible. He would announce his presence at the front door as they broke it down with sledge hammers, thus creating a horrendous din designed to put the fear of God into their victims. The gang would enter a house with candle lamps lit and muskets primed. They pounded on stairways, banged doors, and ran from room to room, discharging a shot or two and generating bedlam and mayhem before accosting their victims. As his notoriety grew and his reputation preceded him, Freney would arrive at a chosen house and simply demand that the occupants admit him. But he never allowed his gang to inflict injury or insult their victims, even when those being robbed tried to defy him or attempted retaliation.

Beefsteaks ~ His Trusted Steed

If a highwayman's life depended entirely on one thing, it was a reliable horse – a horse whose speed and stamina could outpace and outlast any other animal in pursuit of him. Freney had such an animal in his beloved Beefsteaks. He had acquired this young mare as a foal from the Robbins stables, and had trained and prepared her himself for participation in his many sporting challenges at events throughout the counties of south Leinster. Beefsteaks proved to be one of the best and most loyal horses in the country.

As well as catapulting Freney into the limelight as a sporting success, she made him a considerable amount of money from the substantial wagers he placed upon her. He was heard to boast on one occasion that there was nothing in life he loved more than his trusted steed. The mare was always his first consideration, and her needs were seen to before anything else. Freney preached that if you did not have a good horse, you had nothing. A well-trained and obedient horse that understood your commands and was always of the same temperament was essential. It made the difference between life and death to a highwayman – a fact proven by the number of years he operated outside the law.

People who knew Freney and his equine companion were at a loss to say which of them was the more intelligent. The horse was acclaimed as much as its illustrious owner. Freney knew his horse's limitations, and when he was embarking on his most audacious exploits, he planned with this in mind. There were times when he used relays of horses, and on one occasion – when it was essential for him to be in Dublin before word of an outrage he had perpetrated reached the capital – he stationed horses along the route at Bagenalstown, Castledermot and Kill, and by so doing, achieved the outcome he desired.

The name Beefsteaks came about in an unusual way. One day, as he was schooling his young filly, she did not take kindly to the routine and escaped over a fence. She ran wild through the yard before dashing into the slaughterhouse and scattering freshly butchered beef in all directions. As Freney was returning her to the stable, the butcher remarked, 'That nag loves her beefsteaks.' From that day on, the name Beefsteaks stuck.

By the time Freney launched himself on his highway career, Beefsteaks was five years old, and was to be his constant companion during the next three years. The mare was part and parcel of some of his most daring exploits. It was said she had the stamina to travel nonstop for thirty miles, and after resting for a short period of time, could return by the same route with no ill effects.

Her master trained Beefsteaks to understand all his commands

– whistled, signalled and vocal. Many a time, it was her spontaneous intuition that enabled him to evade his pursuers. He never brought Beefsteaks too near to an operation as he was very conscious of the risk of his beloved steed being shot or injured. He trained her to walk backwards for short periods so his pursuers would think that he had gone the other way, and she was used to having her shoes reversed in order to achieve the same result. Wherever he reined her up, Beefsteaks would patiently remain until he returned or gave her some signal to come to him. People said that if he was at an inn or shebeen and a man in a red uniform appeared outside, the horse would neigh in order to alert him to the danger. If this was true, then Dick Turpin's Black Bess was only trotting after her.

But her luck finally ran out. In the late summer of 1747, she developed the staggers, a problem with the central nervous system, and died. Thus ended what was probably the greatest combination of man and horse in the history of Kilkenny and Carlow.

Wake in Kilmanaheen

Finding his finances depleted, James Freney set out one night for Gowran with the intention of robbing the glebe house outside the village. As he approached Bodal Cross, close to Dungarvan village, he encountered a gentleman on horseback and relieved him of fifty gold sovereigns. As he was making his way back to his hideout near Saddle Hill, he passed through the village of Kilmanaheen, a sprawling hamlet a mile distant from Dungarvan, and heard voices up ahead. Thinking that a group of soldiers might be returning to Gowran after spending the day searching for him in the Coppanagh Hills, he pulled up Beefsteaks and listened intently in the darkness to ascertain whether or not they were soldiers. Suddenly, he heard horses coming up behind him. Fearing that more soldiers were approaching from the rear and that he would be caught between both groups, his priority was to get rid of the evidence; getting caught in possession of stolen property would have only one outcome. Dismounting, he removed some stones from the wall beside the lane he was travelling, and quickly deposited the sovereigns therein and replaced the stones as best he could in the dark. As the riders came abreast of him, they bid him good night and enquired of him if there were many at the wake. Freney sized up the situation immediately – a wake was obviously being held locally – and answered that he did not know as he was only passing by and had dismounted to answer a call of nature.

With all the comings and goings of those attending the wake, he could not chance staying around too long as his presence would be noted, especially when word of the robbery got out. He moved on, considering it prudent to leave it until later to retrieve his booty. He passed on through Castlegarden and Cloghsgregg to his retreat near Saddle Hill.

Local tradition says that when word of the robbery reached the village, the wake-goers recalled the chance meeting with the stranger on horseback and concluded that it was Captain Freney himself whom they had encountered. It is believed that he never recovered his loot as he was later seen on many occasions scouring the laneways around the village. It is possible that, to this day, the fifty sovereigns remain unclaimed in that rural boreen. The villagers firmly believed this story, and as late as fifty years ago were often seen searching the ditches and walls in the evening, while claiming when asked that they were collecting kindling to light the fire in the morning. One local man, Johnny McGrath, often told the story about Freney's gold and of his dream of finding it. Sadly, Johnny passed away around forty years ago without realising his dream.

Outwitted in Dunbell

A few nights after the robbery in Kilmanaheen, Freney and his companions entered the home of Henry Anderson – a collector of the hearth tax, who lived in Dunbell. They made their usual entrance by smashing the door and windows with sledgehammers. Anderson was not at home, but had left a couple of burly bodyguards to protect his wife and property. They failed to prove equal to the task, and the felons were soon in control of the house. Freney had been informed that a large sum of rent money had been collected and was kept at the house. He demanded of Mrs Anderson where the money was. She replied that her husband had taken it with him to lodge, and that there was only a trifling sum of change in the house. Freney told her he did not believe her, and that a lady should not descend to such low depths as lying.

The gang searched the house but to no avail. As they prepared to leave with some plate and the little money they had found, Freney enquired of Mrs Anderson if she had any liquor in the house as he was feeling a mite thirsty. She replied that they were strictly teetotal and never kept drink in the house as it led to temptation. Noticing a pail of water, he stepped over to it, cupped his hands together, dipped them into the bucket, withdrew them full of water, and drank heartily. The good lady of the house looked on in panic, as only moments before, she had dropped a pouch containing the rent money – amounting to hundreds of pounds – into the bucket of water. Freney failed to notice the good lady's apprehension, and missed by inches the reward he had come in quest of. He bid her good night, thanked her for her patience and generosity, and said that he was disappointed to have missed Mr Anderson but assured her that he would call to see them again.

It was weeks later when Freney heard the story of his near miss, and it must surely have galled him to find out that he literally had his hand on a fortune and had been foiled by a lady. This story may have put a dent in his growing reputation, and it is reported that he swore that the Andersons would regret having thwarted his intentions.

Wedding at Gowran Castle

A member of Lord Clifden's family was getting married and the wedding celebrations were being held at his country estate in Gowran. Lord Clifden had in his possession a solid gold miniature set of a sow and a litter of bonhams. It was one of his most prized possessions, having been won for displaying the best livestock at an agricultural show, and was one he guarded with the utmost security. Freney was aware of the lord's most cherished treasure, and vowed to relieve him of it.

On the night of the wedding, he made his way to Gowran, and when the party was in full swing, he entered the castle and mingled with the guests. As these were still early days in his new career, no one at the celebration knew him and the guests were unaware that a daring robber was in their midst. He eventually made his way to the chamber where the object of his quest was kept. His luck was in as no one noticed him leaving the reception and he had this section of the castle to himself. He removed the items from the safe, placed them in a sack, slung it over his shoulder and departed the house by a French window. Unknown to him, he was seen by one of the servants as he let himself out the castle. The alarm was raised and the theft was discovered.

Though a search party was immediately sent out to track down the thief, Freney was unaware that his deed had been discovered, and was making a leisurely departure in the direction of Coppanagh. When he realised that a posse was in hot pursuit, he was forced to take a detour towards Neigham – an area that he was not very familiar with – and to head for the safety of high ground. The posse was close on his heels by now, and he was forced to take refuge in Glencoum Wood. Here, he noticed that the posse had split in two and was closing in from both sides. He had no choice but to offload his prize. Having dismounted, he hid it in a stone wall along the boundary of the wood, and considered how best to escape. Being the wily old fox he was, he slipped back in the direction of Gowran in the hope his pursuers would continue to look for him farther away. This they did, and he was able to make good his escape via Dungarvan–Tullaherin.

Some weeks later, Freney went back to retrieve his spoils, but failed to find the wall where he had hidden them – a very difficult task given that this had been done in the dark of night, under pressure of a posse searching for him and in an area with which he was unfamiliar.

Locals in the area believe that Lord Clifden's sow and bonhams are still resting in Glencoum Wood. They recall a time when a local man engaged a clairvoyant to try to locate the treasure. The clairvoyant declared that owing to all the activity in the area by people trying to unearth Freney's booty, her powers of clairvoyance were blocked and she was unable to be of any assistance. It is possible that her crystal-gazing powers were better than she admitted to, and that Lord Clifden's gold ornaments contributed to her early retirement. It is also possible that the treasure belonging to Lord Clifden is still concealed in Glencoum Wood.

Breathless on Brandon Hill

Beefsteaks – breathing heavily – was showing signs of fatigue brought on by the exertion of climbing to the summit of Brandon under pressure. The gap between Freney and his pursuers was narrowing fast. Once again, he found himself in the familiar position of trying to outpace his pursuers and of having to jettison his night's reward. Himself and an accomplice, who had raided a clergyman's house near New Ross, were spotted as they left the scene of the crime. The authorities were alerted and the chase was on. They had been riding along leisurely in the moonlight, on their way back to Inistioge, when they realised that a troop of soldiers was closing on them fast. Splitting up, Freney's companion scuttled towards the village while Freney cantered on, crossed the Nore and headed in the direction of Brandon Hill, hoping to draw the soldiers after him. They took the bait and were soon in full flight as they pursued him through Kilcross and on towards the slopes of Brandon. Beefsteaks kept up a steady gallop, but as they approached the summit, Freney feared he would not reach the River Barrow and safety before the soldiers caught up with him. He decided to dispose of his night's takings.

As he descended from the top of Brandon, and when he was temporarily out of view of the soldiers, he dismounted near a bank of heather and searched around in the semi-darkness for a place to hide his takings. Finding a rabbit burrow, he stuffed his loot inside, concealing it with ferns and stones. He stuck a stick in the ground close to the bank as a marker, remounted and galloped on towards the river. With Beefsteaks getting her second wind while he buried his haul, and with the advantage of the steep descent towards the river, he was halfway there by the time the soldiers reached the summit. They could see him in full flight charging towards the Barrow, and realising he was now out of reach they gave up the chase.

Old storytellers in Graiguenamanagh to this day will tell of Freney returning to Brandon to retrieve his booty and failing to find it. The stick he set as a marker had disappeared, and with so many humps and hollows on Brandon he could not identify the bank that concealed his trove. They will tell you that he made numerous trips to search for the rabbit burrow, but owing to the sheer number of rabbits on Brandon and the abundance of burrows, he was never able to locate it.

However, one morning as the sun was rising, Freney was sitting on a granite rock beside the River Barrow about halfway between Graiguenamanagh and St Mullins, and looking up at Brandon, he noticed a shaft of light reflected in his direction. He knew from the tint of the beam that it was reflected by either silver or gold, and his hopes of finding his treasure rose. On returning to the hill, he again failed to find the correct place as the lie of the land looked very different when he climbed to the spot where he thought the reflected beam came from. Tradition tells that he spent many a morning sitting on the granite rock – now known as Freney's Chair – waiting for the sun to rise and hoping to pinpoint the spot where his treasure lay. Folklore informs us that he never succeeded.

Freney's Rock

At the top of Carrickmourne Hill lies a very large rock. It has been a landmark over the centuries, and holds a commanding view of the Nore Valley. In the days of the bold Captain, it was referred to as Freney's Rock. From here, he kept vigil over the valley and monitored the activities of the local militia as they moved between Thomastown and Inistioge in search of his good self. Today, we know it as Doyle's Rock, it having gained this name from the Doyle family, who owned it over many generations since.

Back in Freney's time, a man died suddenly in the nearby townland of Brownsbarn, and a couple of neighbours volunteered to dig his grave in the family plot in Fossa cemetery. They had dug down about two feet when they were surprised to hear a dull rattle. On removing more clay with their hands, they found a pair of muskets and a leather bag containing a handful of sovereigns wrapped in a greasy cloth. They knew immediately who was responsible for putting them there, and looking up at the high vantage point of Freney's Rock a short distance above them, they saw Freney himself seated on his horse and observing their every move. They expected him to come thundering down to claim their find, but he remained posted in the shadow of a bunch of furze beside the rock, and continued to observe what went on below him. The diggers were apprehensive about what he might do, especially if he thought they were stealing what was his. Suddenly, their attention was diverted to a group of mounted militia coming from the Thomastown direction and who were more than likely out in search of the much-sought-after fugitive.

The captain of the group observed the men in the graveyard and approached them. They covered their find by scraping loose clay over it with their boots as they stood in the grave, and hoped their movements would not be noticed. The troops gathered menacingly around them and demanded to know if they knew anything of Freney – did they know where he was or had they seen him. One of the men, petrified with fear, pointed up to the rock and shouted out that he was up there. All eyes turned in the indicated direction, but nothing could be seen. Freney was no longer visible, and the military thought the grave diggers were making a mockery of them. One of them produced a pistol, pointed it at one of the diggers and demanded that he lie down in the grave to see if it was his fit should he decide to shoot him. He fired two shots into the ground beside the prostate man, leaving him in a state of shock and telling him that if he ever repeated a stunt like that again, he would be a dead man.

The military departed from the graveyard in the direction

of Inistioge. They were scarcely out of view when Freney came galloping up. He scolded the men for having betrayed him, told them they were a disgrace to their country, and said they should hang their heads in shame. He derided them for having no courage, saying that a life lived in fear of the blood-thirsty enemy was a life not worth living. He told the man to get up out of the grave and that he was lucky the Redcoats had not shot him. He made it clear to them that he had much more reason to do it himself. He recovered his muskets, told the men to divide the handful of sovereigns between them, and vanished just as quickly as he had appeared.

Daring Escape at Woodstock

Every morning at six o'clock, the staff of Woodstock House were obliged to assemble in the hallway for a military-style inspection. They stood in line according to rank: kitchen staff, parlour maids, house maids, pantry boys, milkmaids, and so on. As they were preparing to line up one winter's morning, they were startled to see a cloaked figure scuttle across the landing and disappear into a bedroom. The alarm was raised and a search commenced to find the culprit. On entering the bedroom, the searchers found the window open but could see no sign of the fugitive. Hoping to prevent him escaping in the poor light of early morning, they rushed downstairs in order to block off all escape routes around the house. They encircled the house, but failed to catch any sight of the intruder, and concluded that he had made good his escape.

As the searchers were returning to their stations, it was observed that the window of the room through which the thief had exited was now closed, yet none of the staff had any idea who had closed it. On closer examination, it was discovered that the ivy and creeper attached to the house near the window showed signs of having been tampered with. Then the penny dropped: whoever went out the window clung to the creeper and waited until the staff began to search outside before climbing back into the house and making his escape by another route. A thorough search of the house began. While they were searching the servants' quarters, they enquired of a milkmaid if she had seen any strangers about. She replied, 'Only an old beggar woman who was looking for alms at the back door as I went to milk the cows.' The searchers rushed to the back door, but there was no sign of the old woman. It appeared that the burglar had made good his escape via the servants' quarters, dressed as an old woman.

Though nobody had seen the thief up close, they were all certain that it must have been James Freney, as no other scoundrel would have the sheer audacity to enter Woodstock with the intention of committing a felony. As nothing was taken from the house, it was assumed that the morning call-up had spooked him during his attempt at robbery. The owners were thus spared the pain of being parted from some of their most valued possessions.

Just My Size

An encounter on the turnpike road near Burnchurch saw Freney encounter a new breed of rambler – a man who had a gay and carefree attitude to life, and who showed no sign of fear when challenged on the highway. His manner of dress hinted at no wealth; in fact, his whole demeanour suggested poverty. In the twilight of a late summer's evening, when the call of 'Stand and deliver' rang out, the traveller halted and laughingly replied, 'Whoever you are, you are wasting your time. I have not a shilling to my name.'

Freney retorted, 'Let me be the judge of that.'

The traveller dared him to search him. The bold Captain was taken aback at this, and concluded that the nonchalant attitude of this fellow suggested that he was not the full shilling. Freney enquired of him what he did for a living. The man replied, 'Nothing servile. I am a man of words, a master of rhythm and rhyme. I can sling words together like a tailor sews his cloth. But alas,' he continued, 'it brings me no money. I am rewarded for my gift with the necessities of life. The last man I entertained, in his gratitude, gave me this fine pair of shoes.'

He put his foot forward for Freney's inspection. The Captain invited him to take them off so he could see them. He inspected the shoes and decided that they were of excellent quality, having wedge heels and silver buckles. He slipped them on, took a few steps, declared they fitted him like a glove, cast his old tattered ones to the poet, and told him to be on his way. The poet had no option but to put on the tattered old shoes and continue on his journey. Local tradition has it that he put some very uncomplimentary words together about Freney as he bemoaned the loss of his fine pair of shoes.

Turkey Cock at Kilcullen

A wealthy landowner, Mr Rothe, lived in Kilcullen House near Thomastown. Word was out that he had lots of silver cutlery, tableware and gold ornaments in his possession. On hearing this, Freney was eager to pay him a visit and see for himself if this information was correct. On seeing Mr Rothe's coach in Inistioge one evening, he proceeded to his house, hoping to find no one home. As he approached the splendid residence, he saw that the hall door was wide open. He could see no sign of anyone about, so he chanced entering the inviting hallway. As he went inside, he saw a servant girl asleep on a sofa in the parlour. He slid silently past her and collected numerous articles of moderate value. He quickly searched the remainder of the house, but only succeeded in finding two gold watches, some silver candlesticks and a few trinkets of jewellery. He slipped quietly out past the sleeping girl into the dusk of the evening, wondering where was the safest place to hide his loot.

Freney decided to bury it in Mr Rothe's own garden, knowing that he would never think of looking for it there. He found a spade and soon had the lot buried beneath a lilac tree near the centre of the garden. Although he was no stranger to the area, he was not aware of the story that circulated locally that the garden was haunted by an evil spirit who patrolled it at night in the form of a turkey cock. Anyone who entered at night ran the risk of making his acquaintance.

He returned on several occasions and attempted to retrieve his booty, only to be driven off by the marauding bird. The folklore of the area today firmly claims that the contents of the raid on Kilcullen House are still resting in the nearby garden undisturbed.

Bacon in Coolnamuck

Suffering from a very severe bout of the-morning-after-the-night-before sickness, Freney was making his way through the townland of Coolnamuck to a shebeen near the river when he came abreast of a cottier's cabin. Beefsteaks, his mare, came to a stop beside the gate. The woman of the house, a widow, was feeding two pigs in the little yard at the front of the cabin. She recognised Freney and wondered why he had stopped. Thinking that he was gaping at her, she made a cryptic remark something akin to 'Idle hands make the devil's work'. He was not in the best of humour and reacted immediately, saying she was a cantankerous old bitch who should mind her own business and not be casting slight on other people's affairs. She roared back at him that he was a no-good pig, no better than the two she was feeding. His temper erupted at this, as his head was aching and he could not tolerate the sound of her shrill voice. He grabbed his flintlock from beside Beefsteak's neck, took aim at the pigs, and fired. The bigger of the two toppled over in the yard. Death was instantaneous. The widow went into hysterics, ranting and raving, and cursing him. This aggravated Freney more and resulted in the second pig falling victim to his mood. The poor widow went berserk, crying that the pigs were the only thing she had to pay her rent, that she had no money, and that the landlord would evict her. Freney gave Beefsteaks a dig of the spurs and moved on in search of his cure. By this time the widow was down on her two knees, imploring God to strike him dead so that the so-and-so could not inflict any more pain and suffering on man or beast.

Freney continued on his way to get a cure for his sick head, and when his sense of reason returned, his conscience began to trouble him, and the enormity of what he had done and the fear of the consequences of the widow's curse made him have a rethink. He retraced his steps to Coolnamuck and, coming abreast of the cabin, saw a number of men in the yard. They had the pigs dangling from the shafts of a cart and were preparing them for the barrel; the widow was standing at the door still in a state of shock. He reached into his saddlebags, clutched a handful of sovereigns and threw them into the yard, scattering them at the widow's feet, announcing, 'There you are, you old bitch. Now you have your rent and you have bacon,' and continued on his merry way.

This story illustrates a side of Freney that shows he was not the total reprobate some people would have us believe.

St Moling's Cave

After hijacking several wagon-loads of goods belonging to
Waterford merchants on the high road from Mullinavat to
Thomastown, Freney and his gang concealed their loot at
different locations. They hid some in the furze on the high
ground near Castlebanny, some more near Kiltorcan, and the
rest in Ballycocksouis. The more valuable pieces Freney took
with him, and is believed to have hidden them in St Moling's
Cave near Mullinakill. This cave was used by St Moling as a
retreat in the seventh century, and over a millennium later, Freney
used it as the perfect hiding place for his plunder. Owing to its
almost inaccessible location, it was the ideal place for the bold
highwayman to hole up.

As the penal laws were in force at this time, the annual
pattern (feast of St Moling) of Mullinakill was banned and all
expressions of religious fervour were forbidden by law. Owing
to its isolation, some brave souls dared to continue the practice
of the annual pattern in defiance of the law, but mostly it was
felons like Freney who dared to frequent this holy spot. This
cave is almost unknown today, and only a few local people know

of its exact location. Freney was aware of its whereabouts, and often used it to conceal his ill-gotten gains.

It was from near here that he dispatched a ransom demand to the merchants of Waterford, seeking one hundred and fifty pounds in exchange for stolen goods. He lay in wait in the cave for a few days, hoping to hear that the Waterford merchants had agreed to his demand. On the afternoon of the third day, he went outside to relax in the warm sunshine and dozed off. A battalion of troops out searching for the missing goods came near to the spot where he was resting. Suddenly awakened by the sound of the searching soldiers, and believing he was surrounded, Freney silently evaluated his chances of survival. He reached for his primed flintlocks lying by his side. Taking hold of them, he whistled to his mare, Beefsteaks. She came instantly, crashing through the brambles at full speed. The soldiers, startled by the sudden movement, broke lines and scattered to avoid being trampled by the galloping horse. Freney took his chance. He suddenly rose from the ground, threw himself onto her back, blasted off his pistols at the surprised soldiers, and dashed for cover amidst the furze and rocks. The soldiers discharged several volleys after the fleeing figure, but only succeeded in knocking splinters off the trees and furze that gave him cover.

Freney made good his escape on that occasion, only to experience a similar occurrence at Kilmacshane some time later. Here, he faced the ultimate test, and by sheer luck escaped being shot. Reports of his miraculous escapes led people to believe that he had a charmed existence. Like a cat, he appeared to have nine lives.

The Suit of Clothes

One evening, as bold Captain Freney and two of his cronies were drinking in a public house in Thomastown, the need to improve their finances came up for discussion. The Captain had one individual in mind that he had long earmarked for a 'courtesy call': a certain Reverend Collier – a clergyman who lived in Rosbercon and who had been instrumental in preventing him from receiving a suit of clothes promised to him by his employer, Mr Robbins. The clergyman advised Mr Robbins that it would be a far better thing to give the clothes to charity rather than to an employee who had a reputation for carousing and gambling. Mr Robbins informed Freney of his change of heart and the reason for it. Freney immediately formed a strong dislike for the interfering clergyman, and vowed then to have some form of revenge. Now he decided it was time to visit the Reverend Collier in Rosbercon and reimburse himself for the loss of the suit of clothes.

Ten o'clock the next night saw himself and his cronies outside the rectory, ready and willing to execute the task in hand. With their faces blackened and blunderbusses ready, they advanced to the house. Breaking a window with a hammer, they entered and discovered that someone had escaped out a rear window. Freney gave chase and soon caught up with the fleeing figure, only to recognise that the escapee was the rector's wife, whom he had seen in Ballyduff on several occasions. She pleaded for her life, saying her husband was not at home and that he had taken what money was in the house with him. Freney politely assured her she would come to no harm as it was not his policy to insult or be disrespectful to a lady.

He took her back to the house and set about ransacking it. The search provided them with a quantity of plate and silverware, and about seventy pounds in cash. On leaving the house, Freney told Mrs Collier to thank her husband on his behalf and to convey his regrets that they had not met him. Later that night, the gang was heard to boast in a shebeen in Ballyneal that they could afford several suits of clothes owing to the generosity of an unsuspecting benefactor. The Reverend Collier paid a heavy price for having deprived young James Freney of his master's kindness. This episode indicates that Freney could be very vindictive and harbour a grudge for a very long time, and shows that he was a man not to be crossed.

On the Road to Thomastown

One morning, as Freney made leisurely progress along the road from Burnchurch to Thomastown, he was overtaken by a very jolly gentleman who enquired of him if he could ride along with him, as he considered it safer for those using the highway to travel in groups. He was assured by the Captain that he was safe in his company as he would repel any outlaw who tried to take his money. He went so far as to tell his fellow traveller that he had been accosted by the notorious robber Freney on two occasions, and had successfully defied his best efforts to rob him. On hearing this, the man introduced himself, saying he was a Quaker going on a business trip to New Ross, and feared having to travel the highway from Thomastown to New Ross through what he referred to as 'Freney country'. Many of his fellow business associates had been held up by this ruffian and had suffered considerable losses. He said he feared the notorious robber and hoped not to make his acquaintance on this trip. Freney told him that the country was full of robbers and rogues, and that it was not safe for anyone to carry money on their person. He said that he had devised a way to protect his money so it would not be found if he was searched. He told the Quaker that he had false soles on his boots and that he had his money hidden in them.

The Quaker, on hearing this, confided in his new companion that he, too, had a way of defying the robbers: a secret pocket stitched in a position inside his breeches that any man would be embarrassed to consider searching. He put it to Freney that it was a far safer method than his, as somebody might steal his boots. The cunning Captain told him not to bet on it. The Quaker laughed, saying that no self-respecting thief would demand that a man take off his breeches on the highway as it would be an act of indecent exposure. The rogue replied that he would have no qualms about making any traveller take his breeches off on the highway, indecent or not. Alarm bells rang in the Quaker's head, but it was too late. He found himself looking down the barrel of a flintlock pistol and being advised to dismount and to shed his breeches. The Quaker had no option but to do the unthinkable and remove his pants on the roadway. Freney complemented him on the quality of his long-johns, saying that had it been wintertime, he would have gladly requested ownership of the same. He handed the Quaker his own soiled and smelly breeches, and told him to clothe himself before anyone saw him in his state of undress. Having snatched up the Quaker's pants and slipped them on, he felt for the secret pocket that would confirm that his travelling companion was telling the truth. The bulk in the Quaker's breeches told him that he had indeed met a man of substance whose wealth was equal to his word. The Captain told the Quaker that he was too naive and trusting for his own good, and that he was doing him a favour by teaching him a costly lesson. He thanked the Quaker for the trousers, saying that they were of the finest quality and that they were now covering the backside of James Freney.

Later, some verses were put together by a poet of the day to describe the Quaker's trauma on the highway with Freney:

Says the Quaker: It is a friend
His secret unto me would lend
I'll tell you now where my gold does lie
I have it sewed beneath my thigh.

As we rode towards Thomastown
Bold Freney bid me to lie down
Kind sir, your breeches you must resign
Come quickly, strip off, and put on mine.

Says the Quaker: I did not think
That you'd play me such a roguish trick
As my breeches I must resign
I think you are no friend of mine.

Daring Escape at Kilmacshane

Having hijacked a number of carts containing an assortment of goods on the mountain road between Mullinavat and Thomastown, Freney and his gang proceeded to conceal them at different locations in the area of Kiltorcan, Bohilla and Ballycocksouis. He sent the drivers back to Waterford with a ransom demand of a hundred and fifty pounds, payable by the merchants who owned them. At that time, this area of the country was densely covered with furze and brambles, and was ideal territory for concealing anything of bulk from public view. Freney was therefore reasonably sure that they were safe from accidental discovery, and he settled down to wait and see what the Waterford merchants would do.

The merchants notified the authorities and soon the country-side was overrun by Redcoats and bounty hunters of every description. The gang had to make a hasty retreat, and Freney decided to go to his Carlow hideout in St Mullins. He left his hiding place in Ballycocksouis and went down to Kilmacshane, hoping to cross the river to Dobbinsmill and on to Brandon Hill and the safety of his Carlow friends. He observed that all crossing points along the river were guarded by Redcoats and that there was no possibility of crossing until darkness fell. Having decided to lie low and wait, he let his horse loose to graze and settled down to rest in a furrow covered by a briars and furze. The sun was shining and soon he fell fast asleep.

A local man passing with a horse and cart heard him snoring, and thinking that it was an animal in distress, he went to take a closer look. He approached the bushes and, lo and behold, there before him was the notorious highwayman fast asleep. He was aware of the bounty on Freney's head and decided that it was going to be his. He hurried to Inistioge and reported his find to Captain Forrester, and led him and his troops to where the sleeping felon lay concealed. The troops aimed their muskets at the spot the man pointed out, and unleashed a salvo of shots directly into it, hoping to kill their quarry. Freney awoke with a start on hearing the shots and realised that he was under siege. Amazingly, he was not injured, having been saved by the fact that he was resting in a hollow. He looked out through the briars and saw the captain approaching with a musket aimed straight at him. Freney raised his blunderbuss and fired, shooting the captain in the arm. Forrester and his troops backed off hastily. Freney's reputation was enough to have them cowering in fear. Their courage completely deserting them, they withdrew a safe distance to consider their next move.

The captain – holding his badly injured arm – was escorted to Inistioge to have his wound attended to. His plan now was to bring more manpower to surround the fugitive and make sure he was captured him dead or alive. His second-in-command took control and ordered the troops to reload. Being an ambitious young fellow, he considered that it would be a feather in his cap if he could capture Freney in the absence of his superior. He ordered them to advance and fire a second salvo into the break of bushes. Freney's quick thinking came to his rescue. He put his hat on a piece of stick that rested beside him, raised it up at arm's length to the top of the briars and made a rustling sound as if he was attempting to escape. The soldiers fired at and under the hat, expecting to hit the target, but the shots passed over the cunning Freney. He cried out, howling as if in great pain, then let out a few pitiful sobs, gurgled his throat a few times as if drawing his last, and fell silent.

The troops ran up quickly without reloading, thinking that Freney was dead. He burst forth from the briars, roaring that he would kill them all, grabbed the nearest soldier, put his pistol to his head and said he would blow his brains out if the rest of them did not back off. He frogmarched him to the nearest ditch and made good his escape in the direction of the river.

On reaching the river, he found it in flood. Looking left and right to see if there was any place he might attempt to cross, he saw a horse tethered to a bush. He severed the tie, jumped on its back, and throwing caution to the wind, urged it into the raging water in an attempt to cross to the other side. The treacherous current swept them downstream, but towards the far bank, which was most fortunate as the soldiers had reloaded their muskets and were in hot pursuit. On seeing him in the water attempting to scale the bank at the far side, they again sent a salvo of shots in his direction, but he was out of range and successfully made his escape to the safety of Dobbinsmill and Lochingorra Wood.

As they left for Inistioge, Captain Forrester and his escort heard the second salvo being fired and assumed that the highwayman was dead. In fact, they were so sure, they brought a horse and cart back with them to take his body to Inistioge so as to put it on display as a warning to like-minded people what was in store for them if they were tempted to follow in his footsteps. Captain Forrester was to be sorely disappointed when he learned of Freney's escape.

Word spread in the village that Freney had been shot and badly wounded, but that he had escaped. Days later, a rumour spread in the village that he had succumbed to his injuries and was buried by cronies somewhere in Lochingorra Wood. On hearing this news, his gang members pilfered the hidden goods and proceeded to sell them at the pattern of Mullinakill and elsewhere. When a very-much-alive Freney heard of their disloyalty, he sought to call them to order. The hijacked goods by this time were spread all over the place and only two carts remained intact. These he ransomed to the Waterford merchants for what money he could get, returned to his hiding place in St Mullins, and laid low until things cooled down.

Leather Pouch Repaired in Inistioge

Freney was a man ahead of his time. Always thinking of ways to improve his methods for burgling houses and transporting the tools of his trade to and from the scenes of his crimes, he hit on a bright idea for carrying his sledgehammers in a safe and trouble-free way while crisscrossing the country on horseback. He designed a pouch consisting of three lengths of leather each about six inches wide – the longest section being seven feet in length, the other two about three feet each. When laid flat on the longer piece facing inward from the ends and stitched together, they made the perfect holder for his muskets and sledgehammers. When slung over the horse's neck and shoulders, it formed two perfect pouches – each about three feet in length – for holding either sledgehammers or musket.

By inserting the handle of a sledgehammer or the barrel of a gun and pushing those down as far as possible in each pouch, they were ready for use. With the hammer heads resting beside the horse's mane, this brought a perfect balance to the animal and rider, allowing for ample mobility and the freedom to use firearms if necessary.

A story is told by Willie Holden of the Mill Road in Inistioge, of the bold Captain taking this pouch to his great-great-great grandmother – an accomplished needleworker – and requesting she repair it as the stitching was coming adrift. He explained that it was for carrying his muskets and that he would appreciate it if she would attend to it immediately. She did as requested, and was handsomely rewarded for her efforts. Her expertise was very likely called upon more than once, as Freney's rugged lifestyle would surely test any man-made fabric to the limits of its durability.

Hire a Thief to Catch a Thief

Mr Robbins of Ballyduff was very concerned by all the robberies in the area, and feared that sooner or later his own home would be targeted by the burglars. He was advised to hire people to protect his home and property. He knew of only one man whom he was convinced could repulse the robbers and safeguard his house, and that was James Freney. He sent one of his servants to Thomastown to leave word with Freney that he wanted to see him and to come as soon as possible.

The bold Captain – not knowing what was in store – was a little apprehensive as he arrived in Ballyduff. Some time had elapsed since he was employed on the estate, and as his current occupation was at variance with the law, he feared that Mr Robbins might have become aware of his activities and wanted to apprehend him. However, his worst fears were laid to rest as his former employer offered him the post of security man on the estate, saying that he believed Freney was the only man he knew who could guarantee that the robbers would be stoutly resisted and his home safeguarded. This presented Freney with a real dilemma. His father was still steward on the estate and he himself had worked there for many years. The Robbins family had been more than good to him over the years, and he felt obliged to accept the post. It would also provide the perfect cover for his primary occupation, as it would enable the continuation of his thieving habits without the least suspicion falling on him as Mr Robbins' security guard.

Though unintentional, employing Freney to guard his home must have been one of the shrewdest moves Mr Robbins ever made, as there is no record of the house at Ballyduff having being robbed during this period. One would say that it was a classic example of 'hiring a thief to catch a thief', albeit unwittingly.

Freney Contracts Smallpox

In the autumn of 1745, Freney contracted smallpox – a very contagious disease of the skin which, in those days, if not diagnosed early could not be cured. At this time, he was still in charge of security at the Ballyduff estate, and still very much a thief and highwayman.

One evening, the master of Ballyduff, Mr Robbins, informed Freney that the next day he was to go to Carrick-on-Suir to purchase some casks of wine and other goods needed for the house. Carrick at that time was a very prosperous market town owing to its central position between Kilkenny, Waterford and Tipperary. One got greater value for money there than in New Ross or Kilkenny.

On waking the next morning, Freney felt very unwell but duty called, and he set out for Carrick together with a driver and cart. He opted to ride on Beefsteaks in preference to travelling on the cart, as it would be much easier on his aching body. Having concluded their business in Carrick, he instructed the driver to proceed to Castletown, where they had arranged to stay the night with relations of Mrs Robbins. He then retired to the nearest inn to try and relieve his condition with hot whiskeys. Later, he started to make his way to Castletown, but as it was by now early morning, he decided instead to return home.

On arrival at Ballyduff, he complained of being very unwell and retired to bed. Next morning, it was obvious what was ailing him. The 'pox' had broken through, and his upper body and face were covered in a nasty rash. The master, on hearing this, became very alarmed and immediately sent for the doctor. Fearing an outbreak, given the contagious nature of the disease, he had Freney quarantined in an unused section of the house. The doctor arrived and examined Freney. He withdrew and told Mr Robbins that, in his opinion, the condition was too far advanced and beyond medical help, and that it was almost certain the patient would not survive.

Word of Freney's condition spread through the household, and the staff became very apprehensive as they were well aware of the danger of this malady. One of the servants said he knew a quack in Ballycocksouis who had a cure for smallpox, and volunteered to go there and bring him back. On hearing the quack's name, Freney became rather agitated, and said that he doubted that this man would help. He admitted having abused him some time ago when he objected to Freney and his friends hurling in his field of new grass that he intended to mow for hay. The servant insisted that he should ask him anyway. The worst he could do was refuse.

On hearing of Freney's plight, the man agreed to help, saying that Freney's threatening to spread his brains all over the field was no excuse to refuse him aid in his hour of need. On seeing Freney, the quack applied his cure and remarked as he came out of the room, 'Ye have not seen the end of this blackguard yet.'

Somehow, word got out from Ballyduff that Freney's condition was beyond medical aid and that he would not survive. The grapevine accelerated his condition, and word spread that he was dead. To some, this news was the answer to their prayers, as he was the bane of their lives. To others, it was a devastating blow as their knight in shining armour was no more. The members of his gang, on hearing this news, were left in a state of complete disarray. Freney was their commander-in-chief, and deprived of his guidance, they were like a rudderless vessel. Without anyone to plan for them or to direct them, they had no option but to fall back on lesser prey, and began robbing cattle and sheep from the poorer tenant farmers on the hills around Inistioge and Thomastown.

It took Freney over two months to recover from his bout of smallpox, and during his convalescence his gang ran riot, plundering all the smallholders in the area. On hearing of this, Freney was perturbed as it was a complete breach of his code of honour that you 'only rob those who can afford to be robbed'. Freney sent his gang members an ultimatum that they return all they had taken or be accountable to him. Word of his resurrection shocked them, and they immediately did as ordered.

Though Freney recovered, the smallpox left its mark on him. One side of his face was horribly disfigured, and he had lost the sight in one eye. This, however, did not deter him from continuing to cause mayhem among the landed gentry of south Leinster, nor did it affect his ability to shoot straight or judge distances, as is usually the case with a person with only one eye. The scars from this bout of smallpox were to remain with him for the rest of his life, and he wore a broad-rimmed hat to conceal his pockmarked face. It apparently had no long-term ill-effect on him, as some of his most daring escapades were yet to come.

The Cabbagestalk Affair

One evening, as Freney was sitting by the fire at Ballyduff during his convalescence, he overheard a conversation in which Mr Robbins mentioned that his agent was out collecting rents and was due back by nightfall. As darkness was approaching, an audacious plan formed in his mind. He complained of feeling unwell and said that he would go to bed to rest. Having said good night to all present, he retired to his room. Here, he took a blanket from the bed, raised up the window, let himself out onto a roof below and eased himself down to the ground. He was about to retrieve his flintlocks from their hiding place when he heard the clip-clop of hooves coming in his direction, and realised that the agent had returned. Having no time to retrieve his pistols, he had to improvise. Running through the garden in the direction of the oncoming horse, he grabbed a cabbage and broke the stalk from the head. Then, spreading the blanket over himself like a shawl, he positioned himself under a tree beside the gate on the driveway, just as the horse approached. When the agent dismounted to open the gate, Freney, with the cabbage stalk held in his hand like a pistol and disguising his voice, rasped, 'Stand and deliver'. The agent got such a start that he almost fell to the ground.

Freney stole the money from the saddlebags, gave the horse a slap on the backside, which sent him scampering back in the direction from which he had come, and disappeared into the night. The petrified agent, alone in the darkness, had to make his way to the house and report the theft to his master. Freney silently retraced his steps through the garden, returned to his bedroom, hid the booty up the chimney and got into bed. A great commotion commenced downstairs as the agent reported the theft, saying that an old woman in a shawl had held him up with a pistol in the driveway and had taken his money. Freney came downstairs to enquire as to the racket, and the master, seeing him in his nightshirt, never suspected that he could be involved. But Mr Robbins did have a strong suspicion that his agent was less than honest. Freney ridiculed the agent, saying that it was a poor reflection on him to let an old woman rob him, and suggested to his master he should employ a more trustworthy fellow.

Reddy's Innocence

Freney planned a robbery at Derrynahinch to cast doubt as to the guilt of a henchman of his – John Reddy, the man who had originally enticed him to rob on the highway. Reddy was confined to jail and awaited trial for stealing cattle and horses. Whilst held in custody, an added charge of grand larceny was laid against him for breaking and entering at the home of Mr Kendall's steward in Walton's Grove, and for stealing forty pounds. Freney decided the best way to shift suspicion from Reddy was to have a few burglaries occur in the same area while he was incarcerated, thereby convincing the authorities that others and not Reddy were responsible for all the current robberies. Freney chose to rob Mrs Mountford's house in Derrynahinch near Ballyhale.

He enlisted the help of several members of his gang to execute this felony. They employed their usual tactics of smashing doors and windows with sledgehammers, before entering and ransacking the house and helping themselves to a considerable amount of plate, silk, linen and sovereigns. Mrs Mountford and her servants put up no resistance, being terrified for their lives. As all the gang members lived on or near the Ballyduff estate, they decided to bring their considerable takings back with them and hide the lot within the estate, a decision that almost proved to be their downfall.

Panic broke out among the large house owners in the area following the robbery, as they were now of the view that thieves other than Reddy had been responsible for all the crimes they had credited him with. The problem now was to ascertain who the real culprits were. They employed extra hands to guard and protect their properties, and the whole area was on a constant state of alert. Several more robberies were perpetrated around south Kilkenny, which led Lord Carrick to believe that maybe they were targeting the wrong man in Reddy and it was possible that he was not guilty of the charges laid against him. Freney, by this time, had been informed of Lord Carrick's thoughts on the subject, and was delighted that his intervention might succeed in removing the threat to Reddy. However, his work bore no fruit, as Reddy was convicted of cattle rustling and sentenced to seven years in Kilkenny jail.

Treasure in the Pigeon House

Having robbed Mrs Mountford of Derrynahinch of some very fine plate, a quantity of linen and two hundred sovereigns, Freney and his gang took the lot to Ballyduff estate. They buried the plate under the floor of Mr Robbins' pigeon house, with a view to letting it rest there until things died down. They hid the linen in the hayloft as they believed the dampness of the pigeon house would affect and discolour the fabric. Some days later, the linen was discovered by one of Mr Robbins' servants, who then reported the find to the steward who was none other then John Freney, father of the guilty felon. He was unaware of his son's involvement, and reported the find to Mr Robbins. The linen bore the identification marks of Mrs Mountford, and soon the cry was out to catch the thieves. On hearing this news, the bold robber, who was by now in Cork, sent word to his wife to collect the hidden treasure from the pigeon house and bury it in the potato garden, as he knew a full-scale search would be made in Ballyduff.

She did as she was bid, but unfortunately did not do a very good job. The next day, his father, passing by the garden, saw the fresh digging and unearthed the hidden loot. Being a decent man, he reported it to his master, thus confirming his suspicions that locals were responsible for Mrs Mountford's robbery. On hearing this, his wife sent word to James that he was suspected of the robbery and that it would be safer for him to lie low for some time.

Freney absconded to Bristol and remained there for some months, trading in commodities and building up a relationship with the traders there. After a while, his wife got word to him that the Mountford business had died down and that no action was going to be taken as no evidence was forthcoming to connect him or anybody else in Ballyduff to the crime. By this time, he had built up a confidence with the traders in Bristol which allowed him to acquire a considerable amount of goods on credit to export back to Ireland. However, he never paid for the goods, leaving his creditors to deal with a substantial deficit.

The Fury of the
Blacksmith's Wife

News of the notorious gang operating in Kilkenny and Carlow reached Dublin, where Mr Robbins' brother, a King's Counsel, was practising law. His associates derived great satisfaction in telling him that some members of the gang in question were reported to be living on his brother's estate in Inistioge. Counsellor Robbins came home to Ballyduff to inform his brother of this, and demanded to know if he had any idea who they might be. His brother told him that he had suspicions about one employee who was spending a lot more money than he was earning in his employment. This man was James Freney. He said he was attending races, cockfights, hurling matches and card games, and was drinking every night. Naturally, there was a question as to where the money was coming from. Freney claimed that he had won it gambling, and Mr Robbins had no evidence to connect him to any of the crimes committed locally; in fact, he was certain that Freney could not be involved in some of them as he was accompanying himself when the outrages took place. Mr Robbins' brother was not satisfied, and hatched a plan to outwit the rogues. The next day, he paid a visit to an employee of the estate with whom he had grown up and who owed him a very great debt of gratitude. He pressurised him – under the threat of eviction – to take part in a scheme he had devised to trap the criminals. He gave the man several sovereigns, told him to take them that night to the shebeen operated by Moll Burke, and to keep his ears and eyes open. Moll, lived in a small cabin near the entrance to the Ballyduff estate, and sold illicit liquor to supplement her income. The man was to get whoever was there drunk and suggest to one of them that someone in the company had said something derogatory about them. He was instructed to wait for their reaction and to elicit whatever information he could from them.

As instructed, the man went to the shebeen, placed the sovereigns on the table, saying he had found them hidden in a wall, and called for drinks all around. It was not long before those in attendance were merry, and soon everyone was talking freely. The man fell into conversation with an individual named Gaul, whom he suspected might be involved with Freney. After some time, Gaul excused himself to answer a call of nature. The man pleaded likewise, and followed Gaul outside, where he kept him talking for a considerable length of time. They eventually came back inside, and the man left Gaul's company and went to talk to Moll Brophy, the local blacksmith's wife. Moll, a martyr for the drop, possessed a wild streak which, let loose under the influence of alcohol, could turn her into the proverbial wildcat. Moll remarked to him that himself and Gaul had been outside a long time and queried what they had been up to. He told

Moll not to be curious, saying that inquisitive people never heard anything good about themselves. Moll replied that they never said anything good about her anyway, and insisted that he tell her what had been said. With a twinkle in his eye, he told her that Gaul had informed him that she was a woman of easy virtue and that half the men of Inistioge had been to her bed. Moll's inebriated head jerked backwards, fire flashed in her eyes and she erupted like a volcano. She grabbed the brush from behind the door, tore across the floor, and clobbered Gaul on the side of the head, knocking him into a heap on the floor. Gaul, not understanding her fury, pulled himself up, but Moll hit him again, and called him a lying so-and-so, saying he was a-no-good lout who was in no position to cast a slight on anyone's character. She accused him of being a robber and of being a member of Freney's gang. Gaul denied this, only to be lambasted again, and she shouted that she had overheard him telling a friend of his that Freney, Walsh, Grace and himself had robbed Pallister's in New Ross and that Freney had Pallister's gold watch. By this time, the rest of the company had become aware of the fracas, and efforts were made to bring it to an end. Shortly after, the drinkers made their way home.

At first light the next morning, the man went to see Counsellor Robbins to relate to him what he had witnessed the night before. On hearing of what went on at the shebeen, Robbins sent for Moll Brophy and confronted her with what had been reported. Moll venomously denied all, saying that whoever had told him that story was a damn liar, that everybody there was so drunk they could not remember their own name let alone anything else that was supposed to have taken place, and that she had no recollection of anything that he was talking about. Robbins, a man of considerable legal experience, decided to try other tactics. He told her that he would have her thrown in jail for contempt, and would keep her there until she cooperated. He called his coachman, and instructed him to prepare the coach to take her to Thomastown jail. She was put in handcuffs and placed in the carriage, but as they were going down the avenue, she panicked and decided she thought more of her freedom than of Freney's gang, and related the whole episode to Counsellor Robbins. He immediately summoned Captain Forrester, the commander of the local militia, and instructed him to get his troops ready to go out and arrest Freney and his gang. One of the servants got wind of what was afoot and was able to warn one of the gang just in time. Word spread like wildfire, and the felons all escaped to the nearby hills. This episode ended Freney's employment on the estate. He and his gang were declared outlaws, and a reward of five hundred pounds was placed on his head.

Chase on Saddle Hill

Arthur Bushe of Kilfane (brother of Henry Bushe), an earlier victim of Freney, brought in a battalion of soldiers from Kilkenny to hunt down Freney and his gang. He had been informed that Freney was seen near Carrigmourne and was probably on his way to a safe house in Mong. He had high hopes of capturing the wanted felon in the open country around this area – a countryside with which he was very familiar, having hunted over it on many occasions. Bushe had been informed that Freney was holed up with a cottier named Ryan, and was thought to be alone. By the time Bushe had assembled his troops and approached the cabin, it was evening time. They surrounded the house and garden, and called on the felon to surrender. There was no reply. Bushe again called on those inside to come forth. The door opened slightly and a voice called out that they were being held hostage by Freney and that he was in no mood to surrender. Then Freney called out to Bushe, saying that the people of the house were innocent victims of the situation, that he had imposed himself on them, and that he was prepared to release them if Bushe would guarantee that no charge would be brought against them. Bushe agreed and the family was given safe passage from the cabin. As the soldiers prepared to lay siege to the cabin, Bushe again called on Freney to give himself up, threatening to set fire to the cabin if he did not comply. The reply from within was a musket shot through the window in the direction of the troops. Bushe ordered the soldiers to torch the thatch roof, but the straw was damp owing to it having rained the night before, and it did not ignite to any great degree. Rather, it simply caused volumes of smoke to swirl down around the yard.

Opportunity presented itself to Freney. He seized the moment. Opening the door slightly, he discharged a shot outwards. A volley of lead balls crashed through the smoke and embedded in the door. Freney threw open the door, hurled himself out into the yard, and taking advantage of the thick carpet of smoke that enveloped the scene, rolled along the ground. In their confusion, the soldiers discharged shots into the heavy smoke hoping to bring down their quarry, but to no avail. The bold Captain made good his escape under cover of the blanket of smoke, and reached his horse.

Riding bareback, Freney made a furious getaway in the direction of Saddle Hill. Bushe and his troops gave chase immediately, hoping to close down the fleeing felon, but Freney and Beefsteaks outpaced them across the western side of the hill and went in the direction of Blessington. Having neared the brow of the hill, he veered around it and headed back in the direction from which he came. The soldiers, losing sight of him for a period, raced on down the steep incline into Blessington. Realising they had lost their quarry and with night closing in, Bushe decided to call off the search until daybreak. Freney's luck had held out once more, and he went so far as to taunt Bushe and the Redcoats by openly riding through Thomastown the next day, an event they were sure to hear of.

Colonel Pallister of Portobello

The tiny hamlet of Ballyneal nestles in a very secluded rural retreat in the Tullogher/Rosberacon area. Although close to New Ross, it remained a very quiet and tranquil setting, where law and order was held in scant respect. Several shebeens operated in the area, and a number of illicit stills made sure that a constant supply of moonshine was readily available in those unlicensed hostelries.

It was in these lawless surroundings that Freney and his companions spent a lot of their leisure time, and it was here that they planned many of their most daring raids, including that on Colonel Pallister's at Portobello, near Campile in County Wexford. It was well known that the colonel kept large amounts of money in his house, and that he had a selection of valuable plate on display in his drawing room. The colonel boasted that no man would ever attempt to rob him as his home was very securely protected by a band of burly bodyguards. Any man who dared to try would not get out alive. Freney prepared to prove him wrong.

Many obstacles had to be surmounted, including getting

muskets past the guards at the ferry checkpoint before crossing the Barrow, and securing safe keeping for the horses until nightfall. The assault on the house was the culmination of the daring plan, and if all went well, the colonel's burly bodyguards would not present too great a problem. The gang hid their flintlocks, blunderbusses and sledgehammers in trusses of hay, and early in the morning of market day in New Ross, with the hay firmly secured to their horses' sides, they brazenly approached the ferry. Looking the ferry master straight in the eye, they declared that they were going to market to sell their hay. They were ushered on board and were soon safely in County Wexford. They went to a local ale house where they stationed their horses in a livery yard attached to the inn, and settled down to play cards and drink until it was time to go. It was autumn, and darkness descended early. This allowed them plenty of time to put their plan into action.

Nine o'clock saw them approach the Portobello estate, and minutes later they were outside the house. Here, they waited and watched for candlelight to appear in the upstairs windows, which would indicate that the occupants were retiring to bed. It would also identify which room the master occupied. It was common practice in those days for the owners of large houses to place the servants in rooms alongside their own for security reasons.

After waiting for an hour after the candles were extinguished, they decided that the occupants should be fast asleep, and put their plan into action. As usual, they broke down the door with sledgehammers, and generated a terrible din with the sound of smashing timber and splintering glass, with the intention of putting the fear of God into the bodyguards. When Freney announced his presence, the burly bodyguards panicked and retreated to the servants' quarters. Unimpeded, the gang entered the mansion, and stampeded up and down stairways, discharging the odd shot, and causing general confusion and mayhem in the house. They hoped that this would intimidate the occupants into submission. It worked, for they met with no resistance. But when Freney entered the colonel's bedroom, he was met with a stern rebuke, with the colonel demanding to know what his business was at this hour of the night and why was he intruding into a person's private domain. The bold Captain replied that as a visitor he should be accorded a more gracious welcome in the place that his ancestors once owned. The colonel exploded, ordered him to get out, calling for his bodyguards to evict him. Unfortunately, they had proved to be less deserving of their reputation, having fled the scene by the rear door.

Freney snatched the colonel's trousers and watch from the table beside the bed. Searching the pockets, he found a glove containing twenty-eight guineas and some small change. Expressing his disappointment, he demanded to know where the bulk of the money was kept. Now Colonel Pallister showed his mettle. He told Freney there was no more money in the house and invited him to jolly well search if he wished. Freney responded by instructing his troops to ransack the place.

Entering the library, they found a battered old writing desk, which was locked. Freney demanded the key from Pallister, only to be told that it had been lost for years and that the desk contained nothing.

Freney declared he had a very fine key himself, and called to one of his accomplices to bring him the sledgehammer. He split the desk wide open with one stroke, and an assortment of gold and silver coins and two gold watches were strewn around the floor. Freney scooped the coins into a leather pouch, and estimated that there were at least one hundred guineas. He then proceeded to the sitting room where his henchmen had by now collected what plate and valuables they could find in the rest of the house. They had them wrapped in tablecloths and were ready to depart. Their leader went to the sideboard, took out a firkin of whiskey, poured a measure into several glasses, and proposed a toast to the colonel's good health. He then thanked him for his generosity, and said that he admired his courage though not that of his bodyguards, who had failed to live up to expectations. He bid the colonel good night, adding that as his host had been so generous, he might be tempted to call again.

The gang took their leave of the colonel, and on their way back to New Ross they hid some of their loot, so as the bulk would not be noticed as they took the dawn ferry across the river. Having boarded the ferry, they complained of the poor market in town and the lack of customers to buy hay. The ferry master, feeling sorry for them, advised the ferry guards not to harass the poor farmers as they were hungry and weary on account of not being able to sell their goods. Having come from a rural background himself, he understood their plight and felt a tinge of sympathy towards them. Safely across the river in County Kilkenny again – with their weapons and booty secured in the trusses of hay – they proceeded to Poulmonty Wood to share out their spoils. They buried some of their haul in various locations around the wood, and dispersed in several directions. Word of the robbery at Colonel Pallister's house arrived at the ferry too late for the apprehension of the culprits, who were by then safely away.

The possibility of some of this booty still resting in or around Poulmonty Wood has long been a source of speculation. Decayed weaponry was found there many years ago, and this sparked renewed interest in Freney and his gold. Nothing was ever found of the loot they lifted that night at the colonel's expense, but hope reigns supreme in the hearts of some would-be prospectors that they will one day resurrect what remains of Pallister's hidden treasure.

Lord Carrick, a favour returner

Mr Kendall owned the Walton's Grove estate near Thomastown. When a robbery occurred at the home of his agent on the property, Freney was suspected of being responsible for it. A very important portfolio and a considerable sum of money were stolen in the raid. A man on horseback was seen exiting the estate on the night in question and it was generally assumed that the local highwayman, James Freney, had paid a visit to the unsuspecting agent. The portfolio that was taken contained some very important legal documents relating to the title of the estate and Mr Kendall was very anxious to have them returned. He went to see his local rector, Reverend Burke, reported his loss to him and begged him to use his influence to have the items retrieved. Reverend Burke went to see his neighbour Lord Carrick who was a senior magistrate on the circuit and who was responsible for the upkeep of law and order in the area, and demanded that he hunt down Freney and secure the return of the stolen property. Lord Carrick was well aware of Freney's reputation and knew that it was futile to try to apprehend him in open country. He was acquainted with Freney, having come in contact with him when his employer Mr Robbins of Ballyduff house came to visit at Walton's Grove. He held a kindly regard for the likeable young man he had encountered on these visits and hunting him down was not something he would relish on this occasion. He decided to apply other tactics. Through the grapevine he got word to Freney advising him to return the stolen items, and as an enticement he guaranteed a generous reward. The Captain sent back a reply saying that he had not robbed Mr Kendall's agent, but asked if his safety would be assured and he could claim the reward if he was able to restore the lost property. Lord Carrick's answer was yes.

One of Freney's gang, Bolger, had raided the agent's home and as Freney had given no authority for such action he decided to teach his second-in-command a lesson. He confronted the culprit and demanded he hand over the goods. Bolger reluctantly conceded to his request and Freney presented himself at Lord Carrick's that night and handed over the missing property, much to the nobleman's delight. Lord Carrick stood by his word and did not clap him in irons, but thanked him for his prompt response and proceeded to hand over the reward. Freney refused to accept the money, saying that it was reward enough to be of service to his Lordship and that he would pray for his continued good health. As he departed Ballylinch Castle that night he asked his Lordship, if the occasion were to arise in the future where he was in need of help, that Lord Carrick would remember the return of Mr Kendall's property. The notorious felon, who was a far-sighted man, knew the day would come when he would have to call in his favours. History tells us the opportunity did arise when the bold Captain was sentenced to the gallows and Lord Carrick came to his rescue by securing the King's pardon. Various scenarios have been put forward as to why Lord Carrick intervened on the highwayman's behalf and we will probably never know the real reason. But it was said at the time that Lord Carrick was indebted to Freney for services rendered and was returning the favour.

Lord Carrick was later to acquire Mr Kendall's estate and together with his Ballylinch property incorporated them into the now famous Mount Juliet demesne. He built the big house less than ten years after Freney quit the highway and one wonders if the once notorious highwayman ever paid a courtesy call to the palatial home of his gracious benefactor. The former villain dedicated his autobiography to the lord in thankful recognition that he owed him his life.

Riding the Treacherous Currents

In the low-lying area beside the River Nore, below the present Brownsbarn Bridge, a local farmer had collected his hay into several large haystacks in preparation for the coming winter. Unknown to the farmer, Freney had been using one of these large haystacks as a hiding place. Having burrowed into the centre of the stack, he had a secure and warm berth. After three days of torrential rain, the bold Captain was asleep in the dry and warm security of his house of hay when he was suddenly awakened by a gentle rocking movement. On peering out from his hiding place, he discovered that he was surrounded by water and was moving rapidly downriver. A flash flood had come down the valley, carrying everything along with it, including the haystacks, one of which housed the felon. As he took stock of his plight, he was astonished to see a troop of Redcoats coming up the Dobbinsmill road beside the swollen river. He knew that he was the object of their attention, their orders being to apprehend him and bring him to justice.

The haystacks were swept along by the swirling floodwaters. Rocked and rotated by the churning currents, they were rapidly approaching the oncoming soldiers, who caught several glimpses of the helpless Freney within his stack. Seeing the broken branch of a tree floating nearby, he grabbed it and turned it into a paddle and managed to control the cascading stack and turn it around so as to position himself on the blind side of the oncoming troops. As he came abreast of the soldiers, he was now on the aft side of the floating haystack, and they failed to notice him. He swept past them in the raging currents and was carried to the village of Inistioge, where the haystack got wedged against the bridge. Here, he was able to climb to the safety of the road above him.

Today, that same area is liable to flooding after heavy rain, and one wonders if people passing over Brownsbarn Bridge are aware of the life-and-death struggle that took place there so many years ago. Only tradition and folklore reminds us of the time when the gallant rogue navigated a boat made of hay to a miraculous escape from certain death by either drowning or hanging.

Collecting the Eggs

Hungry, cold and tired, the notorious highwayman paid a visit to his uncle's house in Kilcullen to snatch a few hours' sleep and to ease the pangs of hunger that troubled him, as it was a full day since he had eaten. He released Beefsteaks to graze in a nearby paddock, and after a hefty supper of stirabout and potato cake, settled down to enjoy a good night's rest.

Following a tip-off by a member of Freney's own gang, Henry Bushe of Kilfane descended on the area at daybreak with a battalion of troops. As they approached the house, they were spotted by a member of the family who alerted the sleeping felon to the danger. The bold Captain jumped out of bed, and having evaluated the situation, decided to gamble. He took off his pants, put his feet in a pair of *súgán* slippers, put around his waist a *práiscín* (a wraparound apron with a very large pocket in front), pulled a shawl over his head and shoulders, grabbed a rush basket from the dresser, placed his flintlocks inside, went out the door and shuffled across the yard towards the henhouse door. He pushed in the door and the hens fluttered out, cackling in expectation of their breakfast. The Redcoats – who by now had surrounded the house and yard – assumed this was the woman of the house collecting the eggs, and paid scant attention to 'her'. Instead, they focused on the cabin door, expecting the fugitive to make an attempt to escape. Henry Bushe called on the bold Captain to surrender, informing him that there was no escape and that the gallows awaited him. Failing to surrender, he bellowed, would only quicken his demise as the cabin would be burned down around him. Bushe gave the wanted felon an ultimatum to come out or be burned out.

The rogue had by this time made his way out the rear of the henhouse and had summoned Beefsteaks to his side. The Redcoats were startled and surprised when they heard the sound of hoof beats galloping away, and were more surprised still when the fleeing figure of the old lady on horseback discharged two shots at them as 'she' galloped in the direction of Saddle Hill.

Bushe was so frustrated and aggravated at having been outwitted by the fugitive again, that he threatened to torch the cabin over the head of Freney's uncle and his family. However, as he was not the landlord in the Kilcullen area, he had no authority to take vengeful action against the incumbent tenant, and grudgingly withdrew and returned to Thomastown, as pursuing Freney on Saddle Hill had previously proved a pointless occupation.

Bushe returned to Kilfane to await another occasion when he could accomplish the deed he most desired: to capture the notorious outlaw and see him dangling from the gallows. The next day, the wanted felon appeared in Thomastown and rode through Market Street in defiance of Bushe and his Redcoats.

Wake in the Coach House

One night, a concerned citizen or a greedy bounty hunter reported to the authorities in Thomastown barracks that the felon Freney had been seen entering the coach house in Mill Street by the rear entrance. A battalion of Redcoats was dispatched to surround it and to capture him dead or alive. The commanding officer and some of his troops entered the inn and commenced a search for the fugitive. However, the landlord's wife accosted them, telling them that her husband had died and a wake was in progress upstairs, and that it was a desecration and a disgrace to go tearing the place asunder given the circumstances. The officer relented, saying that they would only look into the rooms and not disturb the wake. Meanwhile, Freney had been alerted to the soldiers' presence and realised he was trapped. With soldiers inside and outside the premises, it appeared there was no escape. Everyone in the room was convinced that the bold Captain's luck had finally run out. However, his quick thinking was to save him yet again. With the help of his cronies, he removed the corpse from the bed, stripped it of its waking habit and wig, and heaved it up into the attic space. He donned the habit and wig, rubbed flour on his face, and took its place in the bed. Here he reposed, surrounded by two lighted candles and a bowl of holy water, and with a pair of primed flintlocks under the funeral quilt, while the mourners, mostly cronies of his, knelt around the bed, lamenting the passing of the innkeeper.

As the soldiers entered the wake room, the 'keener' commenced her eulogy. She implored the good Lord and the saints in Heaven to be kind in judgement to the dear departed soul. The Redcoats looked around the room, giving close scrutiny to the mourners. They peered under the bed, gave a passing glance at the corpse – mumbling, 'God rest him' – and left the room to continue their search. After drawing a blank, they paid their respects to the landlady, saying they were sorry for the intrusion and hoped they had not inconvenienced her too much.

Upon their departure, Freney arose from the bed, thanked the mourners for their participation, replaced the corpse in its rightful position, and made a dignified exit into the darkened night. Needless to say, he did not attend the funeral, but word of this exploit was the talk of the town the next day.

The Tailor's Tale

Underneath the foliage of a huge elm tree on the road between Callan and Clonmel was a favourite spot where Freney lay in wait for unsuspecting travellers who came along the highway. He used this vantage point so often that the tree became associated with his activities and was referred to locally as Freney's Tree. The tree is long gone from the scene, and even its exact location is lost in the mists of time.

A story prevails locally of the bold Captain seeing a very well-dressed gentleman approaching from the Clonmel direction. As he came abreast of the tree, the cry of 'Stand and deliver' rang out. Judging by the quality of his suit and the shoes he wore, Freney concluded that this traveller was a well-to-do gentleman, who would be carrying a substantial sum of money. The traveller held his composure and showed no fear of the situation he was in. Freney was amazed at this, as he usually instilled the fear of God in those who stood before him. He demanded that the traveller hand over his purse, and was surprised to see him take a cloth wallet from his inside pocket. Freney felt that his gut feeling had let him down for the first time, as a man of substance would have at least a leather pouch. On opening the wallet, he was even more surprised to find a selection of sewing needles, a thimble, a variety of stitching thread, a cutting knife, a piece of chalk and a few gold coins.

He looked at the traveller with a questioning look, and asked him why he was carrying such things. The traveller replied that they were the tools of his trade: a maker of fine clothes – a tailor – and those were all his worldly possessions. Freney gave him a look of contempt, saying that sewing was a woman's job, and that he would not lower himself to steal from a man of such lowly occupation. 'You will not be robbed by Captain Freney,' he told the traveller, and returned his wallet. But he was curious to know where he got such expensive clothes. The tailor replied that he was rewarded for services rendered with a length of tweed by a satisfied customer and had tailored the suit himself. Freney said that they gave a false impression of his station in life and led people like himself to assume that he was a man of substance.

As he took leave of the tailor, Freney complemented him on his expert craftsmanship but warned him not to mention to anyone that he had been held up by James Freney, perhaps fearing that his reputation for being able to assess a traveller's worth as he approached would be called into question.

This encounter illustrates the mid-eighteenth-century perception of the occupation of tailor, and the episode has been captured in verse:

As we rode a little on the way
We met a tailor dressed most gay
I boldly bid him for to stand
Thinking he was some gentleman
Upon his pockets I laid hold
The first thing I got was a purse of gold
The next thing I found, to my surprise
Was a needle, a thimble and chalk likewise
Your dirty trifle, I disdain
With that I return'd him his gold again.
I'll rob no tailor if I can
I'll rather ten times rob a man.

Archbold of Castledermot

One of Freney's accomplices, when travelling in the Carlow/ Kildare area, gained information that a very large landowner, a Mr Archbold – who also held down a government position – was reputed to keep large sums of money at his home. He conveyed this information to Freney, who decided to pay this man a visit. Freney instructed three of his gang to assemble near Castledermot on a certain night. They proceeded to the stately home, forced entry by breaking a window with a sledgehammer, and sought out the master's bedroom with the intention of persuading him to relinquish his money. As it happened, the master was away from home that night, and only the lady of the house and a servant girl were present. The other servants, who lived in quarters in the courtyard, were unaware of the activity within. Freney forced the locked bedroom door and entered the room only to find the lady of the house curled up under the blankets in a state of distress brought on by all the commotion downstairs. He enquired of her where her husband was. She blurted out that he was away in Dublin on business and would not be back until the following evening. On seeing her distress,

Freney insisted that she would not be harmed, and that there was no need for fear or panic. He assured her that James Freney was a gentleman who had never in his life inflicted injury or insult on a lady. The need of money, he said, was responsible for his presence there that night.

He then proceeded to search the house. On prising open a safe in one of the rooms, he struck lucky. Here, he found three hundred gold sovereigns, a case of jewellery and some gold plate. He returned to the bedroom, apologised to the lady of the house for the trouble he caused, said he was sorry to have missed the master and asked her to convey his gratitude and good wishes to him on his return, and that he would call again to personally thank him. They vacated the house, rode some distance, split the proceeds between them and went their separate ways.

On returning the next day, the master was livid that he had been the victim of the notorious robber. He blamed his servants for not putting up better resistance and swore to double his security in case Freney carried out his threat to return. He announced that he would do all in his power to have the villain apprehended.

Some months later, Freney was travelling alone near Castledermot. Having nothing better to do, he decided to call on what he hoped would be the unsuspecting Mr Archbold. He tied his horse to a tree about a quarter of a mile away from the mansion, and proceeded on foot. As he approached the rear of the Big House, he observed two men standing in a doorway in the courtyard. These, he assumed, were on night watch, so he moved to the front of the house and quietly prised back the sash fastener on a window, raised it up and slid inside. Going to the master bedroom, he found the master and his wife asleep. They were rudely awakened by Freney, and faced his flintlocks. The bold Captain enquired of the master's health, telling him James Freney was at his service and that he had come to pay him a visit. He said he was disappointed to have missed him the last time and expected to be handsomely rewarded for his act of kindness. Archbold's courage failed him. He quietly handed over a leather bag containing two hundred sovereigns and pleaded with Freney not to harm him. The Captain thanked him for his generosity and assured him that he would not be calling again. Bowing to the lady, he bid them good night, but also warned them not to raise the alarm until morning or he would return and burn down the house.

He silently disappeared down the stairs, eased himself out the window and was about to slip quietly away when a dog viciously attacked him, biting him on the calf of his leg. He clobbered the dog on the head with the bag of sovereigns, flattening him to the ground and leaving him for dead. The commotion alerted the watchmen, and they were soon on the scene. Freney dashed in the direction of where his horse was tethered, but the two boys in pursuit blasted off warning shots in the hope of stopping the fugitive in his tracks. Nevertheless, the wily old thief was not to be intimidated.

He reached his horse, and while pulling himself into the

saddle realised that his leg was badly injured where the dog had bitten him. He urged the horse into a frenzied gallop, knowing that a search party would be on his trail immediately. After covering seven or eight miles, he reined up and listened for any sound of pursuing horses that would tell him if they were hot on his trail. When he heard the clatter of hoof beats racing in his direction at a rapid pace, he changed course in the hope of shaking them off. He soon found himself in unfamiliar territory and losing his sense of direction fast in the dark of the night. Worse, he became aware of menacing hoof beats closing in fast.

Suddenly, a substantial ruin loomed up before him, and realising that his horse was tiring fast, he took refuge in its lower quarters and prepared for the shoot-out that would see him either survive or go out in a blaze of glory. To his amazement, his pursers went thundering past, probably thinking that he would not be so foolish as to seek shelter in so obvious a place. He knew that it would not be long before they realised that they had missed him and retraced their tracks. He was also aware that he had to part with his booty, because if he was caught in possession of stolen goods, he would be shot on sight or hanged the next day. Standing on his horse's back and fumbling around in the darkness, he found a hole in the wall, removed some small stones and dry mortar, and pushed the bag of sovereigns in as far as he could reach before sealing it again with the stones and mortar. He then left the ruin and travelled in what he hoped was the direction of Mount Leinster.

After some time, Freney was completely lost, but he had to keep moving in case the searching soldiers came upon him. He travelled for miles, and eventually saw the gloomy shape of a mountain against the dark skyline. He rode on in its direction, but in the night light it seemed to him that he was getting no nearer to it. He eventually came to a wood and decided to rest until daybreak.

First light revealed that he was in fact close to the mountain, and recognising the lie of the land, he was able to make his way safely back to his hideout. Here, he rested for a short while. He knew that it would not be safe to return to try and retrieve his treasure for some time, so he decided to go to England and let things cool down. It was several months before he felt it was safe to return and to search for the ruin in which he had hidden the gold. Apparently, he never located it.

A story circulated in this area many years later seems to verify this assumption. A landowner named Tennent in Ballinkillen, on whose land the ruin of Clowater Castle lay, decided to strip the stones from it so as to use them for various improvements around his farm. He engaged a labourer to do the work, and after spending three days at the job, the labourer came in one evening and asked his employer for the money he had earned, saying he was going to America the next morning. Mr Tennent was astonished, as he knew this man had no money and had never travelled in his life; nor had he ever talked of going to America. He paid the man what he had earned and let him go his way. A week later, he engaged another man to complete the job, and when the stones were all stripped down, he commenced to draw them away. As they were loading the last of the stones, Mr Tennent saw what he thought was a round washer in the loose mortar scattered on the ground. On picking it up, he was amazed to discover that it was in fact a gold sovereign. He continued to search vigorously, and discovered two more. Days of frantic searching after that failed to yield anything. Mr Tennent was well aware of the story of the hidden Freney gold, and was convinced that his first employee – who was by now on his way to America – had found the hoard and absconded with what was rightfully his as the owner of the ruined castle.

Gold on Scalp Mountain

Deep in the heart of beautiful County Wicklow, you will find the bare and foreboding Scalp Mountain. It was in a glen between here and Glendalough that Freney established a hideout. At this time, he was steering clear of Carlow and Kilkenny, and chose instead to carry out a campaign of grand larceny in the unsuspecting countryside of Wicklow, which he knew was ill-prepared to deal with the likes of him. Local lore in this area tells a story of Freney robbing a clergyman's house not far from Glendalough. He escaped with a substantial sum of money, a quantity of plate and a brace of pistols. He was hotly pursued across country and forced to take refuge under Annalecky Bridge. Here, he hid his takings in the river bed.

Near this wild and beautiful spot, he built himself a temporary refuge in a huge sally tree that grew out over the river. This construction consisted of entwined ash suckers among its branches, laced together with ivy to form a base, and covered with rushes to protect him from the elements. With the tree in full foliage, it offered him ample cover from those who passed nearby. He is said to have spent a number of months in this area, and his presence there is still recalled today by the numerous stories told of his daring raids on the homes of the landed gentry, in what is now known as the Garden of Ireland.

In a secluded glen on the eastern side of Scalp Mountain lived an acquaintance of Freney's, and it was in his cabin that the bold robber spent many a day while he waited for the furore to subside after he committed some of his outlandish robberies. As he sat in the kitchen one evening, he noticed that the rays of the setting sun as it dipped behind the mountain, shone through the kitchen window and were reflected by a silver dish on the dresser back onto the shaded mountainside. The idea struck him that where the shaft of light hit the mountain would make an easily identifiable spot for hiding his takings. That night, he carried out a robbery on an estate agent whom he had been told had a very considerable amount of hearth tax money in his home. His luck was in, and his capture amounted to almost three hundred pounds, a selection of quality plate and two very fine gold watches. The next evening, he waited on the mountain as the sun was setting, and where its reflected rays hit the hillside, he buried his takings, secure in the knowledge that whenever he wanted to retrieve it, all he had to do was wait for a sunny evening, and the reflected rays would pinpoint the exact spot for him. He was certain that this method of identifying the spot was much better than placing a stick or a pile of stones there.

Two months later, he decided it was safe to recover his haul.

He went to the mountain and waited for the sun to set. He began to dig where the shaft of light hit the hillside, but to no avail. He dug in several places close to the beam of the reflected sunlight, but could not find his booty. He suspected that his accomplice had helped himself to the stash, and he went to demand retribution. His crony shuddered in fear and swore on the Bible that he knew nothing of the money, but the Captain had his doubts.

However, it was Freney's lack of knowledge of the solar system that had caused the problem. He was unaware that the sun moved marginally to the south or the north each day depending on the season, and that he would have to return on that exact day a year later in order to hit the spot where his booty lay buried.

Freney's hoard may still be buried on the side of Scalp Mountain, and if the day of the year and the exact location of his accomplice's cabin was known, gold might once again be found in the Wicklow Hills.

Wicklow Blunder

Focusing his attention on the mansion of a wealthy landlord near Glendalough, Freney approached his objective late at night. His scouts had informed that the militia in the local barracks were about to be relieved, and he reckoned that they would not be as focused on their duty at that moment. Forcing the front door open, he was confronted by half a dozen soldiers in their night attire. He was not aware that the mansion had recently been vacated by its owner and was now occupied by a battalion of Redcoats. Quick thinking was called for. He pretended to be drunk, saying that he was attached to the relief battalion that was due to replace them in a matter of days, that he had been on leave and celebrating with friends locally, and that he was now coming to rejoin his comrades.

The soldiers fell for it. They took him to the kitchen, where they tried to sober him up before bedding him down for the night. After some hours, he crept from the room, helped himself to a couple of soldiers' uniforms, a gold watch and a brace of pistols that hung by the doorway, and disappeared into the night. Next morning, the commander was so incensed and embarrassed by the brazen robbery that he swore he would not rest until the culprit was apprehended and swinging from the gallows.

Freney knew that the pursuit would be relentless, leaving him no option but to get clear of the area and not return. He buried his capture on Scalp Mountain and made his way to the safety of his hideout at St Mullins back in County Kilkenny. Local tradition believes that he never again ventured back in search of his Wicklow haul. The soldiers spent a week trying to locate the culprit, but to no avail. He had vanished like a morning mist, and it was days later when they discovered that their visitor that night was none other than the bold highwayman, James Freney. This hidden treasure may still be hidden on Scalp Mountain, but local lore speculates that a tenant sheep farmer struck it lucky there about a hundred years ago, and it is suggested that he enjoyed the company of a gold timepiece well into his twilight years.

There is a postscript to this story: the bold Captain is reputed to have robbed a magistrate's house near Carlow town wearing a soldier's uniform that more than likely bore a Wicklow insignia.

The Blackstairs Mountains

The Blackstairs Mountains occupy a gloomy and forbidding landscape when approached in the fading light of late evening. Imagine trying to make your way down the steep rocky incline of the rugged peak known as the White Mountain, in the depth of wintertime. A thick, murky blanket of cloud usually descends upon the mountain as night approaches, and makes it all but impossible to negotiate the hostile terrain. High up on this barren peak, you will find Caher Roe's Den, a hideout used by the notorious horse thief, Charles Dempsey – known locally as Caher na gCapall. Freney used this same hideout for more or less the same purpose a short number of years after poor Charles had met his end swinging from the gallows. One immediately understands why James Freney chose to establish a base in this godforsaken spot: all the armies on earth would not find you here. When the mist and fog descended, it was the ideal place for a man on the run to hide out.

The Blackstairs are renowned for their rugged beauty and the cold biting weather that one is exposed to there during the winter months. They have kept watch over the boundary of Counties Wexford and Carlow since time immemorial, and anywhere from Glynn to Mount Leinster would have suited Freney's purpose. Tradition in the area recalls that he spent a lot of time here, and numerous sites are mentioned as having offered the beleaguered highwayman sanctuary and a place to hide his booty. But unless you know them like the back of your hand, you would have little chance of survival here. The bold Captain was well acquainted with this desolate landscape, and his knowledge of the mountains often stood him in good stead. The Blackstairs are only a stone's throw from Brandon Hill and the Coppanagh Hill, and the towns of New Ross, Enniscorthy, Bunclody, Bagenalstown, Gowran, Kilkenny, Thomastown, Graiguenamanagh and Inistioge were all within easy reach. Freney was a meticulous man who planned his operations down to the last detail. He was a firm believer in the saying, 'Knowledge is power and a little thereof is a dangerous thing'. He firmly adhered to this motto, and always did his homework by acquainting himself with the lie of the land where he intended to operate.

Supernatural Experience in Cluan Castle

Late one night, as the bold Captain was returning from New Ross on horseback, along the river bank to Lochingorra Wood, the sky suddenly darkened and a ferocious electrical storm broke out. Gales raged, the rain fell in torrents, and flashes of lightning lit up the whole countryside. The thunder rumbled and its sound reverberated all around him. He had no option but to take shelter, and the only source near at hand was the notoriously haunted ruin of the once beautiful Cluan Castle. He entered the eerie and forbidding ruin and settled down to wait until the elements had run their course and the storm abated. Lightning illuminated the whole castle with every flash, and he could see clearly the outline of the interior of the ruin. Suddenly, he realised he was not alone. He saw before him a luxurious room where a banquet was in full swing. The guests were seated and toasting the master, who sat at the head of the table. Then a tremendous bolt of lightning hit the room, splitting the walls asunder, and the roof came crashing down, engulfing all at the table. Freney could hear the pitiful cries of those trapped in the collapsed room, and the whole building vibrated to the roar of the ensuing thunder. An eerie silence descended on the scene as the spectre before him faded away before his eyes in a haze of mist.

Terror gripped him as he realised that the scene he had witnessed was not of this world. Suddenly, the silence was replaced by the sounds of the raging storm again echoing in his ears. Even the courage of the bold Captain could not withstand this experience, and he vacated the castle just as quickly as the lightning bolts that passed around him. He, who scoffed at the notion that the other world at times mingles with our own, was left in no doubt that the legend of Cluan Castle was more than just an old wives' tale.

Had a curse blighted Cluan Castle? In its glory days the castle had been the seat of the powerful Fitzgerald family, and its peer was known as the Baron of Cluan. A cruel and heartless man, he had tortured and murdered the son of a poor widow woman, who on hearing of this desperate deed went down on her knees and cursed the baron. It is said she implored both God and the devil to put an end to his cruel reign, and to banish his family from Cluan for ever. It is believed today that this curse led to the extinction of the once great Fitzgerald line. The castle, having been struck by lightning, was reduced to a ruin and all within its walls were killed. The widow's hope that the magnificent castle would one day be reduced to a ruin and only play host to the wild animals of the fields and the birds of the air, seems to have come to fruition.

Outfoxed and Outwitted

On a wet and rainy fair-day morning, just outside the town of Graiguenamanagh, Freney accosted a traveller on the Raheen Road. The traveller, on his way to the fair, showed some annoyance at this interruption, and lambasted Freney, saying that he was a lout, too lazy to work, and living off the backs of God-fearing people. Freney, taken somewhat aback and with his ego slightly dented, dismounted from Beefsteaks and moved up close to the furious and agitated man. He pushed his blunderbuss up to his chest and ordered him to dismount. The man grudgingly obeyed. Freney squared up to him, and demanded that he hand over his money. 'You'll have to shoot me to get it,' was his quick response. The bold Captain gave the fellow's horse a slap on the rump that sent it cantering away up Coolroe Hill, and again demanded that his victim deliver up his purse. The unfortunate fellow had no option but to comply. He put his hand inside his cloak and withdrew a bulging pouch from within. Freney reached to grab it, but as he did so, the frustrated traveller whirled about and hurled it over the ditch and into the field beside them.

Freney was furious at this turn of events, and as he negotiated his way over the ditch to retrieve the purse, he admonished the man for his blatant stupidity. Freney searched about in the early-morning dawn for his coveted prize, and on finding it discovered that the pouch was full of shingle. His frustration mounted as he realised that he had been duped, but it quickly turned to sheer anger when he heard his victim ride furiously away on Beefsteaks, his cherished mare. The fleeing traveller must have felt somewhat elated at the thought of having outwitted the wily highwayman.

Two sharp whistles from the Captain's lips brought Beefsteaks to a screeching halt, catapulting the unsuspecting escapee into the dyke beside the road. As he pulled himself out of the water-logged trench, Freney caught up with him and began to search his clothes, but no purse or money could he find. The sound of people approaching on their way to the fair fell on the Captain's ears, so he decided that the prudent thing to do was to vacate the scene. He mounted Beefsteaks and sped away towards Coppanagh Gap.

The bedraggled wayfarer was delighted to see the early-morning fair-goers come to his aid. He explained his predicament to them, saying he had been held up by Freney and that their arrival on the scene had saved him from the thieving scoundrel. He told them that by frightening his horse away, the rogue had unwittingly outfoxed himself. His money, he told them, was in the saddlebags attached to the horse, and he enlisted their help to round up the animal along the Raheen Road. This they duly did, and returned to attend the fair.

The man was the toast of the town that day, and by evening had attained the status of local celebrity as word spread of his encounter with the notorious highwayman. It appears that by scaring the horse away, Freney was the architect of his own undoing on this occasion. This lucky traveller was one of the few to escape a financial deficiency after encountering the wanted felon on the highway.

Eviction in Brownsbarn

A widow woman, Mrs Cody, who had a large family and who rented a cabin and a few acres of land at Brownsbarn from the Ballyduff estate, found herself in arrears of rent to the tune of thirty pounds. This amounted to two years' rent and, with no possible way of paying it, she was in danger of eviction. Mr Robbins, the landlord, had felt sorry for her plight, and had prevented his agent from evicting her on two occasions. His agent was a cruel, callous and calculating man, and told Mr Robbins that if he allowed this to continue, the other tenants would soon follow suit and he would have a very grave situation on his hands. Mr Robbins recognised the logic of the argument, and with great reluctance allowed him to take whatever action he deemed necessary to resolve the situation. The agent immediately went to the widow and demanded she pay up or be evicted. She told him she did not have any money, and begged for more time. He showed no mercy. Alighting from his horse, he nailed an eviction notice to her door, saying she had three days to clear her debt. The alternative was to vacate the holding, and if not, she would be forcefully removed.

Word of the impending eviction spread like wildfire, and everyone in the area was soon aware of the widow's plight. Most were willing and ready to support her in any way they could. On the eve of the eviction, neighbours assembled at the widow's cabin and prayed to God for a miracle. They told her not to worry; they would see to it that she had a roof over her head, and assured her that God would provide for her.

Later that night, the widow heard a knock on the door, and on asking who was there, was answered, 'A friend'. She slid the timber beam back from behind the door and opened it slightly. In the dark, she barely recognised Freney. He came into the kitchen, sat by the fire and asked the widow about her situation. She told him she owed thirty pounds in back rent and had to pay a few other small bills in Inistioge and Thomastown. He said he would lend her the money and she could pay him back whenever she had it. She swore that as sure as God was her witness and as long as she had a breath in her body, she would return the money. He took out a leather purse and counted out forty sovereigns on the kitchen table. He told her she had enough there to cover her rent and had a few pounds extra to tide her over. She said she would go and settle with the agent first thing in the morning. Freney said, 'No. Let the agent and his bailiffs come to the house, and just as they are about to break down the door, hand out the money to them.' He told her all the neighbours would be there to protest and condemn this action and agitate against the agent and his troops. He told her scuffles and violence could erupt, as this was the usual pattern of events at an eviction. The widow got down on her knees and thanked him with all her heart, and said it was an answer to her prayers. As he went out the door, he glanced back, saying, 'Pray woman, and say one for me.'

Ten o'clock in the morning – the usual time for an eviction – saw the agent and his bailiffs approaching the cabin. A bunch of agitated and aggressive protesters had already assembled in the yard, and were in a very hostile mood. Vibes of suppressed anger and resentment were in the air, and erupted into a chorus of gibes and catcalls when the agent called for his rent. On getting no reply, he ordered his bailiffs to break down the door. They assembled the battering ram and were preparing to charge the door when a barrage of stones descended upon them. They dropped the ram, grabbed their bayonets, and charged at the assembled throng, dispersing them in all directions. The agent called them back, hoping the show of strength was enough to dampen down their hostile mood, and instructed the bailiffs to proceed to break down the door. As they mounted the ram to make the charge, the door opened slightly and the widow handed out the money to the nearest bailiff and closed the door swiftly again. The bailiff handed the money to the agent who counted it and put it in his saddlebag. Disappointment was written all over his face at this turn of events, as he was looking forward to demonstrating his power of attorney to the assembled mob. He turned his horse with a jerk of the reins and gave a gruff command to the bailiffs to return to barracks. Facing the angry mob was something he did not relish, and he decided it was best to make a quick exit, leaving his bailiffs to run the gauntlet of hostility as they collected their artillery to return to base.

The agent had to ride to the ford at Dobbinsmill to cross the river on his way back to Ballyduff. As he entered the water, he saw a horse and rider approaching at great haste from the other side, then plunge into the river, sending water cascading and splashing in all directions. The agent's horse, being of a flighty nature, took fright, reared up on its hind legs and dislodged him into the swirling water. Caught unawares, the agent let go of the reins as he fell. The oncoming rider grabbing his horse's reins was the last thing he saw as he slid beneath the water. On surfacing, he caught a glimpse of the rider disappearing with his horse and saddlebag in the direction of Lochingorra Wood.

That night, the widow received another visit from Freney, who told her that there now was no need for her to repay him the loan as the kindly agent had reimbursed him earlier in the day. He handed her another five sovereigns, telling her to be thrifty with her money as it was unlikely he would be available to help her out again, were the occasion to arise.

Stories similar to this are told in many townlands from New Ross to Thomastown, and if only a fraction of them are true, it is not surprising that the folk memory of the flamboyant highwayman has transformed from that of notorious and dangerous robber to lovable rogue.

The Siege of Freney's Den
at Lawcus

Travellers on the Waterford to Kilkenny road often attracted the attention of the wily robber. Some of his most daring highway assaults took place just outside Stoneyford village on the Kilkenny road, near the old toll bridge at Ennisnag.

A barren plot of land beside the King's River, a short distance south of the old bridge, which was sheltered by a ledge of solid rock, made the ideal lookout for Freney. This narrow strip of land was used by the brazen robber to corral his horse while he waited for some unsuspecting wayfarer to come along. His frequent usage of this plot eventually saw people refer to it as Freney's Den, a name it bears to the present day. He kept his horse fully saddled at this small space, in preparation for the chase when the opportunity presented itself. A ledge jutting out from the upper section of this rocky terrain gave shelter to the highwayman from the elements, and afforded him protection from sudden attack. The river ran parallel to this rocky outpost, which also protected him on his north-western flank. From his perch, he could survey the toll bridge and the roadway in both directions for a considerable distance. With his telescope he could observe the coaches as they stopped at the bridge, and determine how many were on board before he decided to make his assault. He waited until the coaches had passed well clear of the toll bridge before he moved in, knowing that he would have completed his task and left the scene before help could arrive. Coach drivers and passengers alike were always apprehensive as they approached this location, as they expected to see a rider in full gallop clutching a blunderbuss in his outstretched hand hurtling towards them. They were only too well aware that such a sight spelled trouble for them, and would serve as a first warning that they were about to be requested to surrender their cash. Freney became such a menace on this highway that many of the coach owners employed an outrider to proceed along the route ahead of the coach so as to warn of anything that might spell danger. It was here that Freney robbed a coach that included among its passengers a female relative of Captain Wemyess of Danesfort – the commander of a battalion of militia in Kilkenny – and Wemyess declared outright war on the outlaw.

One of Captain Wemyess' informants sent him word a week after the robbery to the effect that Freney was holed up in his den above the toll bridge. Wemyess organised his troops, split them in two groups, and instructed one lot to go to Bennettsbridge and proceed to Stoneyford via Norelands and close in on the fugitive from the village end. The remaining group he took with him along the Waterford road with the intention of making an all-out assault on the fugitive and either capturing him, shooting him dead or forcing him to flee in the direction of the village. He hoped that the two groups of soldiers would form a net around Freney, and that the unsuspecting thief would be sandwiched between them, leaving him with no option but to surrender or die. As the operation got underway, the weather deteriorated rapidly and the rain began to fall in torrents. As the soldiers approached their quarry, the evening twilight was setting in and visibility was reduced to some twenty paces or less as they surrounded the rocky outpost. The highwayman, who was sheltering under the protruding ledge, sensed the approaching danger. In the fading light of the dying evening, he could see the mounted Redcoats closing in all around him, some coming along by the river from the bridge and more approaching from the high ground at his rear, and more still coming along the river bank from upstream. He crept over to Beefsteaks, removed his muskets from the pouch that hung around her neck, replaced them with two long sticks, bound them together with a strand of creeper, draped his cloak over them, and tucked it in under the rear of the saddle. He fixed his hat on top of the longer of the sticks so it appeared in the darkness that a rider was on board. He pulled himself up into an ivy bush and discharged a shot in the direction of the oncoming soldiers. The startled mare took flight and stampeded at full gallop along the river bank. The approaching soldiers were taken by surprise and moved aside to avoid been rammed and trampled by what they thought was the escaping felon. Self-preservation was the first order of the day as far as they were concerned. In their efforts to avoid a collision, they failed to fire at the oncoming target, and only after he passed did they manage to deliver a strike. Some of the soldiers on the high ground fired directly at the fleeing felon, and delivered a salvo of musket shot into his back. They were certain that they had inflicted severe damage, as they had fired at what they were convinced was the escaping robber and had concentrated their aim directly at the figure in the saddle. All the missiles passed directly over Beefsteaks and she escaped unhurt.

The soldiers were speechless at what they were witnessing – that a man could absorb so many hits and still remain upright. They gave vigorous chase in the darkness and caught up with Beefsteaks on the Kells road. It was here that they discovered they had been duped by the wily rogue, and the damaged cloak showed that it had indeed taken a number of direct hits. The soldiers returned immediately to search for the cunning felon, who had by now disappeared into the night. They blamed the teeming rain and failing daylight and the foolishness of making an assault at night for their failure to capture the elusive Freney. As they departed Ennisnag, returning to barracks with Beefsteaks tethered at the rear, a shrill piercing whistle rang out over the night air. Beefsteaks moved backwards, pulled her head from the tethered bridle, and disappeared into the night. The bold robber had again survived against all the odds, and had his own resilience and presence of mind to thank for the freedom he still enjoyed.

Impersonated at Friarshill

Drinking one winter's evening at the Coach House Inn in Mill Street in Thomastown – a hostelry that still continues to cater for the people of the town – Freney and a few of his cronies were interrupted by the sudden entrance of a gentleman in an agitated condition, declaring that he had been robbed by Freney just outside the town. He told them that he was an agent collecting some overdue rents and was returning to Lord Carrick's with the money. He was in a very disturbed and frustrated state of mind as he contemplated the reaction of his employer on receiving this bad news.

Freney approached him and asked if he was certain that it was the notorious highwayman who had robbed him. The gentleman replied, 'Definitely, he told me he was Freney.' The bold Captain asked him did he know Freney. The rent collector said that he had seen him at sports events and races a few years ago, but had never actually spoken to him. The Captain suggested that as the rent collector had only seen Freney at a distance, he could not be sure that it was he who had robbed him, especially in the dark of night. It could have been somebody claiming to be Freney. The rent collector agreed that this was possible.

Freney enquired of him whether there be a reward if the money was returned to him. The agent said there would be. The Captain enquired how much. 'Five sovereigns,' said the agent.

Freney said, 'Make it ten and I will see if I can recover your money.'

The agent agreed, thankful for any help that anyone could offer. The Captain went back to his cronies, and warned them not to divulge who he was. Then he departed by the back door.

The bold highwayman had a very good idea who was responsible for this outrage. He knew of only one man who had the audacity and sheer neck to pass himself off as Freney. That was a member of his own gang by the name of Grace. He rode straight to Grace's cabin a few miles south-east of the town, burst in the door, and sure enough, there was Grace with the leather purse still in his possession. Freney swept the purse from his hand, put his blunderbuss to his face and told him that if he ever pulled a stunt like that again, he would blow his brains out. The Captain admonished him for the impersonation, saying the only good thing to come out of it was that at least his reputation was still intact.

Freney returned to the inn and handed the purse to the rent collector, who counted its contents, making sure that it was all there. With a smile returning to his face, he handed Freney the ten sovereigns as agreed, and thanked him profusely, saying if only everyone was as honest and honourable as he was, this would be a better world. He enquired of Freney his name, but the reply was evasive. Freney said he was just a knight of the road who was pleased to be of service to a gentleman like himself. The bold Captain then bid him good night and left by the back door.

The rent collector, anxious to know the identity of the man who had saved the day, questioned the innkeeper, only to be told that the most notorious highwayman he was ever likely to meet – James Freney – had just been at his service.

Close Call in Ballycocksouis

Under the cover of darkness is when most villains strike, and such was the case when one of Freney's henchmen – Nash – sold him out and a military ambush was put in place for him as he returned to Nash's home in Ballycocksouis after a night's drinking. Freney considered Nash a friend and his cabin a safe haven. The Captain had been drinking all night and was in no fit state to defend himself, so the advantage lay on the side of the military.

Freney had got the loan of a horse from a friend to go to Inistioge to meet some of his gang and spend the evening drinking and playing cards. As he was returning to spend the night in Nash's house, the soldiers lay in wait for him. But as he approached the house in the pitch dark, the horse, being of a flighty nature, was startled by the clicking sound of the Redcoats cocking their muskets. The animal bolted, leaving Freney hanging on for dear life. It galloped at full speed along the laneway. The soldiers, surprised by the sudden acceleration, fired rapidly into the darkness at the fleeing horseman, hoping to bring him down. A number of shots hit the target and inflicted severe injury on Freney. The horse took him to safety away from the soldiers and circled back in the direction from which they came. The Captain urged the horse on in the direction of the river, hoping to cross to the safety of Lochingorra Wood. They negotiated the river and made it to the safety of the familiar wood. Here, he realised that he had been shot several times, in the thigh and the back of his leg. His hat was blown off and he suffered a severe graze on the side of his head. The fact that he was drunk acted as an anaesthetic, and he did not realise the full extent of his injuries. He abandoned the horse and dragged himself into his den deep in the heart of the wood, and fell into an alcohol-induced sleep.

On waking the next morning, Freney realised that his injuries were extensive. He could only walk with great difficulty and his whole body ached. He knew that if he did not have the lead removed from his wounds, he would die an agonising death from blood poisoning. He dragged himself to the house of one of his henchmen some distance away, and medical aid was summoned for him. Recovery was slow. In the meantime, word of the ambush got out, and news circulated that he had been severely wounded, had died of his injuries, and was buried in either Dysart or Lochingorra Wood.

Freney spent several weeks convalescing between Denn's Wood in Dysart and Clonemuck Wood near Tullogher, which he reached by paddling down the Nore at night. It is believed that Nash received a bounty from Arthur Bushe of Kilfane for betraying the wanted felon. News of Freney's demise spread like wildfire, and the gentry were delighted to have seen the last of the thieving robber who had plagued them.

Some three months later, when fully recovered, Freney appeared in Burnchurch and word spread just as quickly of his resurrection. This was bad news indeed for those who thought they had seen the last of him. The task of apprehending and bringing him to justice would have to begin again. After this humiliation, Arthur Bushe, Lord Carrick and the Earl of Bessborough combined forces to bring an end to his reign once and for all. For weeks, they searched the country high and low – on Brandon Hill, Saddle Hill, Cullintra Hill and in every wood from Lord Desart's to Clonmuck – but no trace of the elusive Captain could they find. They picked up some of his cronies, but owing to lack of evidence and gilt-edged alibis, they were unable to bring charges against them and the men were released.

As these searches were in progress, Freney appeared in Inistioge and Thomastown, much to the annoyance of Arthur Bushe and the others, who considered Freney was playing games with them and making a mockery of their efforts. After this, the Captain lay low for a while, and it is believed he spent a few months in Hull in England, only to appear in Kilkenny a short time later and resume his activities, to the consternation of all at large.

Treasure in Burnchurch

After raiding a house in Kilkenny city one night, Freney and a few of his henchmen made their way to Maddockstown with the intention of breaking into the home of Mr Collis, who at that time was one of the richest men in the county owing to his extensive marble works. On arrival, they found the family still up and entertaining friends, so they decided to leave it for another time. They crossed the Nore at Warrington ford and made their way to Burnchurch. Here, in a disused quarry, they shared out the night's takings and went to their respective homes.

The Captain had arranged to stay in a safe house nearby, so he decided to bury his share in the soft gravel in the quarry floor with the intention of retrieving it prior to his departure for home. Providence intervened, and he found himself engaged in a three-day drinking-and-card playing binge with the occupants of the safe house. Word of his presence in the area got out, and soon the local militia organised a posse to apprehend him. The local bush telegraph informed Freney of the approaching danger, and he had to beat a hasty retreat, leaving his booty buried in the quarry. The military continued to search the area for some days, so returning was out of the question until he was sure it was safe to do so.

When Freney did return to the quarry to retrieve his loot, he found that a huge bank of clay and gravel had collapsed down on the spot where he had buried it, and there was no hope of recovering it. Local lore says that a certain individual in the area found the treasure while digging in the quarry one hundred years ago, but no one is able to confirm the authenticity of this claim. A local man, who acquired a metal detector a few years ago, was seen on many occasions scouring the quarry in the hope that Freney's gold was still there. We will never know if he had any success, but a story like this assures us that the legend of Freney still lives on in the hearts of hopeful prospectors in and around Burnchurch.

The Widow's Luck

The sound of sobbing fell on Freney's ears as he approached Danesfort on the Burnchurch road. He had come upon the aftermath of an eviction. A woman and her two children were huddled in the ditch beside a gateway that led to the smouldering shell of what was once their home. He did not have to ask what had happened. He had seen it all before. He recognised with a glance that they were an unfortunate family on the receiving end of a heartless landlord. They looked a sorry sight, clinging to one another in the ditch with their sparse few chattels scattered beside them. He reached his hand into his saddle bag, took out a fistful of sovereigns, and offered them to the pitiful wretch who cowered before him. She thanked him profusely, saying that it was the hand of God that sent a soul so kind along, as she and her two children had nowhere to go and had no one to look out for them as her poor husband had passed away two years before. She said she had fallen behind with the rent. No mercy was shown her. Eviction followed, and her pauper's cabin was burned to the ground to prevent her and her children going back indoors to shelter from the elements. Freney enquired from her the name of her landlord. She answered, 'Captain Wemyess.' He replied that it was time that he paid him a visit, to show him the error of his ways. She was trembling as she told him that there was no point going to plead her case as her landlord was a harsh and evil man, and would give him no hearing. Freney said that he was not going to plead her case, but this was – patting his blunderbuss hanging by his horse's neck. The poor woman shrieked in terror, thinking that he was going to confront the landlord at gunpoint on her behalf. Freney told her not to worry, saying it was his intention to call on the good gentleman for some time as he had some business of his own to square with him, and now was as good a time as any. The woman enquired of Freney who it was that had come to her aid. He replied that he was a 'knight of the road' who God had sent her way. If ever she heard tell of a horse named Beefsteaks, then its illustrious owner had helped her on her way. Whether he ever paid a visit to the said gentleman or not, we do not know.

Freney and the Fairies

On several occasions, the notorious outlaw claimed to have had encounters with the 'little people'. He was one of the few courageous souls who would venture to enter their private domain, the fairy *rath*. Many times, he hid the proceeds of his robberies in the outer surrounds of ring forts, full sure in the knowledge that it would remain untouched there. Belief in the fairies and the superstitions attached to them was so strong, it assured him that no one would venture into a fairy *rath* for fear of being abducted. Such was the fear and respect held for the little people among the general population, that mavericks like Freney were able to play on this superstition and turn it to their advantage. On several occasions he boasted of engaging in hurling matches with the wee folk, and lauded their skill and ability to engage in the national pastime.

One moonlit night, as he was digging in the outer bank of a ring fort to bury his loot, he was suddenly aware of the sound of excited voices. A troop of very small people made their way from within the fort to a level patch of ground a short distance away. Here, as if by magic, a pair of goalposts appeared at either end of the plot, and the excited fairies began to puck a ball around the pitch. He backed away, hoping to get out without being seen. He was apprehended by a wizened-looking old gent dressed in the quaintest of clothes, who, addressing him in a commanding voice, informed him that one of the opposing team had not turned up and he would have to take his place. Freney knew better than to protest, and meekly followed the old leprechaun onto the pitch. He was drafted onto the team and informed that his very life depended on his performance. He was told in no uncertain manner that failure resulted in the losing team being banished from the fort and never being allowed to return. The game commenced and the ball was propelled from one end of the field to the other, and returned as quickly. It continued in this manner until half-time, with no score being registered. Freney, feeling the effects of his efforts, realised that the little people were no pushovers. Kicks from their pointed shoes and strokes of the clashing hurleys left him in considerable discomfort. He was very apprehensive about what might happen in the second half.

However, the wily rogue knew a lot about the wee folk, and his knowledge was about to be put to the test. The second half progressed much the same as the first, and as the game approached full time, the teams were still locked in scoreless combat. Freney grabbed the ball, dashed up the field and dragged the ball through a recently dropped cow dung that lay on the short grass, covering it completely in a messy slime. He had heard that the fairies abhorred the stench of fresh cow manure, and he was about to put this theory to the test. He ran up the field towards the opposing goal and directed the *sliotar* straight at the goalkeeper. The poor fairy, stifled by the stench of the flying dung bag, could not find it in himself to stop it, and Freney registered the only score of the game. When full time blew, he was carried shoulder high around the pitch, and was being taken into the fort when he realised what was happening. He wrenched himself free from the throng and ran full belt to where he had left Beefsteaks tethered to a *skeagh*. As he reached for the reins, he went crashing to the ground, having run into the hole that he was digging beforehand to hide his loot. At that very moment, the moon was covered by a black menacing cloud, and everything was plunged into total darkness. Having regained his composure, he realised that an eerie silence had descended on the scene. Missing was the cheering throng, and the goalposts had vanished as mysteriously as they had appeared. Freney, though feeling very disorientated, managed to mount his horse and got out of there as fast as he could.

The next morning, in the clear light of day, he tried to recall the events of the night before. The facts were muddled in his confused mind, so he decided to return to the fort to see if he could find any evidence of what he thought had taken place the night before. On arriving at the fort, nothing looked out of place. The hole he was digging was there – unfinished and with the booty he intended to bury lying beside it. He was starting to believe that he had imagined it all or that he was the victim of an unscrupulous shebeen keeper who had served him some under-matured poteen. Then he remembered the cow-dung incident, and went to the area where he thought he would find it. Sure enough, what remained of the cow droppings was there, plastered into the grass and showing every sign of something having been dragged through it. This was the only evidence he could find of what he thought had happened the night before, and which went some way to proving that the episode was not a figment of his imagination.

Many people at that time firmly believed that Freney had the luck of the fairies and that he had been touched by a leprechaun. This was a distinct possibility, as he definitely handled a lot of gold and had more than his share of luck. Some believed that he made his own luck, which is probably nearer to the mark, while others concluded that it was a case of the 'devil's children having the devil's luck'.

Retreat at Killenaule

Jim Keane, who lived near Burnchurch and who was reputed to be a member of a gang of sheep robbers, came into contact with Freney and informed him that a man named Watson, a large land owner who lived near Killenaule, had sold a considerable amount of stock and kept his money in his home. Freney decided that he would strike while the iron was hot. Assembling his gang, he prepared to pay Mr Watson a visit. Some members of his gang were a bit apprehensive about this excursion, as there was a rumour that Watson had devised a system of defence that would repel any thief who was brave or foolish enough to try and gain entry to his house. The grapevine had it that he had installed a guillotine system that consisted of scythes suspended on pulleys which dropped down when the door or windows were forced open. Freney was not deterred, and admonished his accomplices for their lack of courage. He and the gang then proceeded to Killenaule to make an assault on the unsuspecting Watson.

On arrival at Watson's house, they commenced breaking down the hall door with sledgehammers, announcing that

James Freney was about to enter. Watson, who was ever vigilant, was prepared for this eventuality, and was soon repelling the assault. As they broke down the door, the intruders were met with a barrage of musket fire from the landing over the stairs, and had to hurriedly withdraw. They returned fire from outside the doorway, which only resulted in a portion of the bannister being blown away. Freney, not being used to such resistance, roared out that he was going to burn down the house around them unless they ceased fire. Watson retorted that neither he nor any of his gang would leave this place alive if they persisted with the attack.

Freney calculated Watson's exact position at the top of the stairway from the sound of voice, and estimated that he could get a shot at him through the rear window of the landing and reclaim the upper hand. He grabbed a musket from one of the group whose job it was to prime and charge the pistols after each volley was discharged. He rushed to the rear of the house, took aim at where he believed Watson was standing, and pulled the trigger. However, the musket exploded in his face, and the hammer was propelled backwards before becoming embedded in his cheek, causing a very serious injury and momentary blindness. The musket had been over-primed in the hurry, and Freney had paid the price. His injury left him with no option but to withdraw. With the help of his henchmen, he retreated from the scene.

Watson had proved to be a tougher opponent than Freney had estimated, and was one of the few to escape the wrath of the notorious robber. He was said to have boasted in Killenaule the next day about how he had repelled Freney and his henchmen. He said that they lacked courage and were found wanting when their bluff was called. He claimed to have out-gunned Freney and forced him to retreat. Only Freney and his gang knew that the intervention of Divine providence had played a major part in Watson's claim to fame.

The assault on Watson's house proved to be one of the few occasions where Freney failed to accomplish his mission, but like all good operators, he took heed of the lessons learned and never again was the gang found wanting when it came to priming a blunderbuss. He intended returning to Mr Watson's to teach him a lesson in humility. However, more pressing matters decreed that Mr Watson's claim went unchallenged, leaving Freney's reputation badly sullied. This failure was something that caused him anguish and regret afterwards, especially as he never got the opportunity to turn the tables on the wily Watson.

Mount Loftus Revisited

John Eaton – the owner of Mount Eaton estate, now known as Mount Loftus – was making his way home early one morning after spending the night playing cards. Eaton had the reputation of being a heavy gambler, and on occasion would be carrying large sums of money after a productive night's play. As he approached his home along the tree-lined avenue that led past Drumroe Castle, he was startled by the rasping command of 'Stand and deliver'. The dark and sinister form of a man on horseback moved out from underneath the trees to block his way along the avenue. As he moved nearer, Eaton could make out the menacing shape of a blunderbuss pointing directly at his chest. Dawn was breaking, and Eaton could see that the man before him resembled the dreaded highwayman James Freney. He knew that there was no way out but to surrender his money. He handed over his pouch, gold watch, silver snuffbox and his silver tankard. Freney accepted the offered items, opened the leather pouch, fingered the stash of coins, and estimated that it contained at least two hundred sovereigns. He said to Eaton that it was a very fortunate night for both of them as each had apparently had a lucky strike. He handed him back a handful of sovereigns, saying that it was their stake in the next card game, and that he looked forward to a profitable partnership. Eaton and Freney, he said, would make a formidable combination.

Eaton's patience exploded at this arrogance, and he ranted and raved about seeing Freney dangling from the gallows. Freney rode away laughing, saying that if an Eaton could get him to a hangman's rope, he would gladly slip the noose around his neck himself. 'On second thoughts,' he called out, 'it would be much nicer still to see the noose around Eaton's own neck.'

On his way back along the river bank at Ullard, the bold Captain decided it would be prudent to hide his loot, knowing that if a felon was caught in possession of stolen property, the punishment was death by hanging. Local tradition varies as to the exact spot he chose to conceal it. Some say that he buried it near St Fiachra's well, while others claim that it is a short distance away in the old graveyard that contains the high cross. Either way, all agree that the stash was more than likely recovered many years ago, when a certain family in the area showed signs of sudden affluence.

Ullard is located roughly halfway between Borris and Graiguenamanagh, where it nestles on the bank of the Barrow and would have been an ideal spot for the bold Captain's requirements. It offered him protection and safety along the river, thus eliminating the risk of sudden capture as the Redcoats could only approach from its western flank. Freney is fondly remembered in Ullard today, and his many exploits there are recalled with relish. His robbing Mount Loftus with the shoes on his horses turned backwards is a favourite tale, and his many crossing points along the Barrow can still be pointed out today.

Drag Artist

Being sought in every corner of Counties Carlow, Kilkenny and Kildare, Freney was forced to lie low. He split from his gang and went into hiding, but his persistent pursuit by the Redcoats gave him no peace. The authorities in the three counties combined to hunt him down, and carried out such a relentless search that they forced him to move further afield.

He contacted a friend in Waterford, a ship's captain, and arranged his passage to the Isle of Man. The ship sailed from Waterford, and as it rounded Carnsore Point, a ferocious south-easterly gale blew up, forcing the ship first towards the Welsh coast and later – as the wind changed to the east – forcing it back to the Irish coast. The storm took control of the ship and battered it relentlessly for hours, but by sheer luck, it was carried into Dublin Bay, and the captain succeeded in taking her into the safety of the harbour. The ship had to remain for weeks to affect repairs.

As it was too dangerous for Freney to remain for long periods in any one place – especially Dublin – the ship's captain was anxious to be rid of him, fearing he would be discovered on board, resulting in the impounding of his ship or worse. The captain suggested that he disguise himself in women's clothing and pose as his fiancée, and that they hire a carriage to take them to Kilkenny. If challenged, they would say they were eloping. Leaving Dublin in the dark of early morning, they travelled southwards. Freney complained that the women's shoes hurt his feet and the corset that constrained his bulging stomach was biting into his flesh. The captain told him to stop complaining, it being better to put up with a little pain than be dead.

Kill in County Kildare was their first scheduled stop. Here, they would exchange horses and have some breakfast. Disaster nearly befell them as they were getting out of the coach. The landlord came out to meet them and insisted on helping the lady down from the footboard. Freney, fearing detection, feigned a fall and complained of injuring his leg. The captain took his hand, fussed over him, and helped him into the inn. Freney hobbled along, hoping the landlord would not notice his pockmarked face and discover that he was not a woman. However, his luck held out in Kill, and his pretence succeeded.

Fearing that the driver might notice his disguise in the light of day, Freney suggested to the captain that he should ply him with drink, and then drive the coach themselves to Castledermot. He was anxious to avoid Naas and Kilcullen as one of his henchmen was held in Naas jail, and he suspected that by now he may have divulged all to the authorities, implicating him in the robbing of Archbold's near Castledermot. He was anxious to get to Carlow, fearing searches on the road, and felt certain that if he could reach Ballinabranna, he would be safe. As they approached Carlow, it was just nightfall. Having reined up the coach, Freney changed back into his own clothes. They placed the merry driver back in the driving seat, and gave one of the horses a slap on the backside, sending them scurrying in the direction of the coach house. Here, they parted company – much to the captain's relief. He set out on his way back to Dublin, and passed through Carlow town and on to Ballinabranna without incident, eventually making it to a safe house near Gowran.

Henry Bushe, when informed that Freney had escaped by sea from Waterford, gave up his search, thinking that he had seen the last of the troublesome highwayman. But after lying low for some months, Freney was back in action along the highways and byways of his beloved Nore Valley.

Candle in the Window

Arthur Bushe of Kilfane and the local militia swooped on the cabin of one of Freney's henchmen, Martin Millea, who lived in the area between Jerpoint and Ballycocksouis. They hoped to find the felon holed up there, but their luck was out as Freney had moved on only hours before. Bushe pressurised Millea, telling him that if he lured Freney to his home so that they could capture him, he would see that no charges would be brought against him over accusations of horse stealing. Millea refused, as his fear of Freney was much greater than his fear of Bushe. He also knew that there was very little evidence against him, as the horses were never found. Bushe then tried a different tactic. He offered Millea ten pounds as an enticement to get him to agree to set Freney up. Ten pounds was a very considerable sum of money at that time, and must have been very enticing to a man who would not earn it in a year. However, he still refused, and only when Bushe raised it to sixteen pounds did his resolve weaken. He arranged with Bushe that the next time he came across Freney, he would invite him to his home and insist that he stay the night. It was arranged that he would send word to the barracks in Thomastown when he had the unsuspecting felon in his company, and that he would place a lighted candle in the rear window of his cabin to confirm that Freney was inside.

While drinking in Thomastown one afternoon some weeks later, he bumped into Freney. After several hours of heavy drinking, Millea suggested to him that they go home to his place for something to eat and to spend the night. Freney told him that he had no horse and had no way of going or getting back. Millea insisted, saying that they could both ride on his horse, and that Freney could have the loan of a young and gallant grey mare he had at home to take him back the next day, and could keep it as long as he wished. Freney agreed. Millea then excused himself to answer nature's call, and told Freney that he would be back in a short while. Once outside, he quickly made his way to the barracks and informed them that the scene was set.

It was dusk by the time they arrived at Millea's house, and after eating, Freney – who had a foreboding that something was not right – said to Millea that he was anxious to be on his way, saying that he feared that someone might have seen them on the road and reported them to the militia. He said he did not want to get Millea into trouble and that if they found him in his home, they would burn it down. Millea reassured him that no one had seen them, and insisted he stay the night. He would even put people on guard outside to warn them if anyone came about. He told Freney that there was a bed in the garret and he could sleep there. The bold Captain's sixth sense alerted him to the fact that something was amiss. He sensed that Millea was too insistent that he stay. He asked Millea to get the mare for him, so he could be on his way. Millea again insisted that he stay, but Freney refused, saying that he would not impose on his hospitality any longer, and was very grateful for the kindness shown him.

Millea knew Freney too well to try anything untoward, so he agreed and said that he would send a boy out to catch the grey mare. As the lad was going out to get the halter, Millea went with him and instructed him to catch the old broken-down mare belonging to his father, and to delay as long as he could. He knew that the troops would be along any minute, and that even if Freney got away on the old mare, she could not outrun them. While Millea and the boy were getting the halter, Freney looked into the bedroom and saw the lighted candle in the window. His gut feeling urged him to get out of there as quickly as possible. He primed his blunderbuss and had it at the ready under his cloak. It was pitch dark when the boy came in with the mare, saying he could not find the young horse and brought the older one instead. Freney mounted the mare, and as he was going out of the yard, he crouched down along her back, fearing that Millea might shoot him as he left. To his surprise, a volley of musket shots rang out from up front, and the mare collapsed under him, having received the bulk of the assault. Freney rolled to the ground, grabbing hold of his blunderbuss as he fell. He took refuge behind the fallen animal and waited for the attack he was sure would follow. He heard the soldiers reload their muskets, but to his surprise, none approached. He heard one proclaim that the villain must be dead, calling for a candle lamp to verify this assumption. Freney fired his musket in the direction of the voices, and scampered away in the dark. He escaped to a nearby field and followed the ditch to safety. The shot he fired had stopped the soldiers in their tracks, and they were reluctant to follow him into the night. His reputation had instilled fear in their hearts, and even the bravest soul could not find the courage to pursue him.

Arthur Bushe and his troops suffered the indignity of being outfoxed by the villain again, and Millea had to seek refuge with a distant cousin for fear of the terrible retribution that he knew for sure would follow from Freney. However, when it came, it was from a different source, as he and several members of Freney's former gang were convicted and executed for crimes committed against the state.

Surgery on a Traitor

Several of Freney's gang were apprehended by Counsellor Robbins' troops and coerced into revealing where the fugitive was hiding. They were also forced to spy on him, and in return were guaranteed that no charges would be brought against them in the event of his capture. The bold Captain got wind of this, and decided to make an example of one of them to demonstrate what would happen if they continued to supply information to Counsellor Robbins. Freney visited the house of a certain Walsh, who was passing on information on the location of his hiding places to the local militia. He burst into his cabin, grabbed Walsh by the hair, put a knife to his throat, and declared that he was dead meat. Walsh admitted his treachery, and begged Freney not to kill him. Freney gave him an option: lose an ear or lose a leg. Walsh begged for mercy, saying that he would never betray him again. The bold Captain took hold of his leg, jerked it up on the table and plunged a knife deep into the soft flesh of his calf. Walsh roared in pain and begged for mercy, but Freney told him he had plenty of practice at this type of amputation and that under different circumstances would have made a very fine surgeon. Another member of the gang arrived on the scene and interceded for Walsh. So Freney offered to shoot him instead. Picking up his primed blunderbuss, he fired a shot so close to Walsh's ear that it singed the hair on the side of his head, causing him to collapse on the floor in a faint. When he came to, Freney told him to consider himself lucky to be still alive, and instructed him to go tell the priest in Inistioge that he, Freney, was not responsible for the outrages that were committed in the area. He warned him that failing to do so would result in him having his brains spread out over Ballycocksouis.

The priest had no great love for Freney. Fearing repercussions from the militia, he had denounced Freney at Mass, saying that anyone who gave him food or shelter would incur the wrath of God, and that he could not give them absolution. He considered Freney and his gang to be the cause of the Redcoats harassing his parishioners and wreaking havoc in the area.

Freney's gang began to break up as trust had broken down among them and each member was suspicious of the other. Time was running out for the gang, and like drowning rats they began to abandon the sinking ship. Freney now realised that the end of this way of life was in sight, and that only drastic action could save his life. The wily old warrior was equal to the challenge. He offered to surrender to Counsellor Robbins, and succeeded in securing a truce while they agreed the conditions of his surrender. The conditions demanded by the counsellor were not acceptable to Freney, and the negotiations broke down without having reached agreement. The demand that he give evidence against his henchmen was unacceptable to Freney.

The relentless pursuit of him began again, and he and his second-in-command, Bolger, found themselves isolated from the rest of the gang, with very few friends prepared to give them sanctuary. With the militia hounding them, and given their constant fear that gang members would either shoot them or inform on them, their options grew fewer and fewer. Time was running out for them, and Freney had to consider his wife and family. He was aware only too well that his luck could not last forever.

The Timber Bolts

Two members of his gang, John Walsh and Tommy Grace, were apprehended and charged with breaking and entering the home of Mr Archbold near Castledermot, and stealing an amount of cash and plate. They were convicted and sentenced to the gallows. While they were awaiting execution in Naas jail, Walsh got a member of his family to go to Dublin and plead with Counsellor Robbins to intercede on his behalf, and to request a pardon be granted in exchange for information on those who were responsible for all the crimes committed in County Kilkenny. He assured the counsellor that he could provide him with the names of those responsible and the locations of where they had committed their, and that he was prepared to swear on the Bible to this effect. The counsellor called to Naas jail to hear at first hand what Walsh had to say. He also interviewed Grace on his arrival at the jail, but the only information Grace would give him was on two members of the gang who were already in jail and awaiting trial. However, Walsh turned out to be much more informative, and related a full account of all the gang's activities to the counsellor.

The counsellor was now in possession of some solid information, and contrived a plan to capture Freney. He instructed Walsh to send word to Freney that he had discovered that the windows of the jail were held in place by timber dowels driven through the framework, and could be displaced very easily by sawing through them from the outside, thus enabling the removal of the window. He pleaded with Freney to come and break out the window that they might have their freedom. The bold Captain, being the wise old owl he was, sensed entrapment. Knowing that no jail of any merit would have timber bolts holding the windows in place, he declined to go to their assistance, pleading that his physical condition prevented him from travelling such a long distance. The counsellor's plan had failed, and needless to say, Walsh's pardon never materialised. He was taken to Kilkenny to swear evidence against the rest of the gang. A hung jury saw the gang acquitted.

Lord Desart's Wood

In Burnchurch and Cuffsgrange, County Kilkenny, Freney had a lot of contacts, and some of his most trusted lieutenants came from this part of the county. On one occasion, when he was staying in what he considered a safe haven, he was alerted to a group of militia marching in the direction of the house. Seemingly, his trusted lieutenants were not as trustworthy as he thought. As the soldiers approached the yard, Freney made a sudden dash from the house, catching them by surprise. He managed to get to his horse and make a clear getaway. The soldiers gave chase immediately. Lord Desart's Wood was only a short distance away, and he was certain that if he could reach the safety of this canopied fortress, he could elude any pursuers. As he came within sight of the wood, he was horrified to see another group of soldiers galloping towards him from that direction, thus cutting him off from the safety of the wood. He reined up and looking back, realised he was trapped, with soldiers closing in fast from both sides. He had no option but to face the charging troops.

Freney raised his hands shoulder high to await the inevitable.

The soldiers were very wary of their quarry, as they were only too well aware of his reputation. They circled him at a safe distance as he continued to sit on his horse. His hands still raised, he called out to the commanding officer that he realised his position was hopeless and he had no option but to surrender. The commander of the troops, Captain Wemyess, began to ridicule him, saying he was a coward who was afraid to die, and that the mighty had become the meek. Freney replied that he was a realist and knew when the odds were stacked against him, and that any other course of action on his part was useless. He informed the captain that he was an Irishman and a rapparee who considered himself at war with the establishment, and as such was entitled to military consideration, namely, that under the code of government regulations involving surrender, it was military practice that the vanquished submit only to the officer in charge. Freney invited the captain to ride up to him alone to accept his surrender. Captain Wemyess agreed to this, safe in the knowledge that his quarry was surrounded and firmly held in range of his soldiers' muskets.

As he rode up to Freney, he was anticipating promotion and visualising the honour and praise that would be heaped upon him for the capture of the most notorious outlaw this side of Dublin city. He was in such a state of bullish elation that he did not even take the precaution of having his pistol at the ready as he moved in to accept the surrender. Suddenly, he was looking down the barrel of a flintlock pistol that Freney had produced from the sleeve of his cloak. The bold robber stuck the muzzle into the captain's jaw, told him to call off his troops, and insisted he be given clear passage to the wood or he would blow his brains out. Wemyess' courage failed him as he realised his predicament. The crafty rapparee had turned the tables on him, leaving him no option but to command his troops to fall back. Freney grabbed the captain's reins and urged the horses towards the boundary of the wood. Here, he relieved the good Captain Wemyess of his pistols, his sword, his gold watch and the money he had to buy refreshments for his troops. As he retreated into the safety of the wood, he told the captain to consider himself a lucky man that he was not going to meet his maker that day, and that he owed his life to a man of honour who never shot anyone in cold blood. He then bid him good day.

Freney disappeared into the bosom of Lord Desart's Wood, leaving the bewildered captain to face the mockery of his troops and the scorn of his superior officer when they returned to barracks. Freney's decision to attempt the impossible and succeed illustrated an ability to astutely evaluate any given situation, and a reckless courage and sheer audacity to gamble with his life.

The Shooting of
Sheriff Henry Burgess

The fugitives Freney and Bolger were holed up in what they considered a safe house near Lord Desart's estate on the old Callan road, not far from Cuffsgrange village. Other members of the gang had informed Sheriff Burgess in Kilkenny where they could be found. The sheriff and his troops surrounded the house, and decided to rush in and surprise the wanted felons. They expected that they would not give up without a fight.

The sheriff barged through the kitchen door, discharging his musket as he entered. The commotion woke Freney in time to see Bolger firing his musket at the oncoming Burgess, who collapsed clutching his chest. The soldiers dragged him clear of the door, but it was evident that he was seriously wounded. The soldiers retaliated by setting fire to the thatched roof over their heads, but Freney and Bolger escaped in the cloud of smoke that enveloped the cabin as the fire took hold. Shots were discharged in all directions by both parties. By the time the soldiers caught sight of the fugitives again, they were at the end of the yard and almost out of range. They fired a salvo of shots after the fugitives, and one hit Bolger in the thigh as he scaled a wall, severely wounding him. Freney had to assist the injured Bolger to make the safety of Desart Wood.

Bolger was so badly wounded that he could not continue, and he urged Freney to go on alone. Reluctantly, Freney did, but only after settling Bolger down in cover and promising to send help. Bolger was picked up by the soldiers the next day after a ferocious struggle, and lodged in Kilkenny jail. Unfortunately for him, Burgess died from his wound and he was charged, tried and convicted of the murder, and sentenced to be executed that very day.

As a warning of what would happen to like-minded people, his tortured remains were hung on a gate beside the road near where the crime was committed. His severed head was spiked on top of the gate, and a number of soldiers stationed there to prevent anyone removing it in order to give him a Christian burial. However, during the night, the remains were somehow removed, despite the presence of the soldiers, and disappeared without trace. Local tradition has it that Freney succeeded in removing it from right under the soldiers' noses, and that he took it away and buried it in an unmarked grave somewhere on Lord Desart's estate. Once again, the bold Captain displayed his reckless courage in outwitting the detested Redcoats, and proving they were no match for the indomitable spirit of a freedom-loving Irishman.

The Net Closes In

When he realised that members of his own gang had sold himself and Bolger out, Freney knew that it was only a matter of time until he was captured or shot. With Bolger's execution, he found himself completely alone and unable to rely on his many safe houses, which left him with only one option: retreating to the hills. He believed that in order to survive, he would have to submit. He got a family member to approach Counsellor Robbins to negotiate terms for a conditional surrender, requesting a pardon be granted in return for information on the whereabouts of members of his gang. The counsellor was in no mood for negotiation, saying that Freney had been given an opportunity before and had spurned what were considered very favourable terms, and gave him an ultimatum that he surrender forthwith. The counsellor assured him that then, and only then, would he request his superiors to consider the granting of a pardon. Freney decided that he could not continue under his current circumstances, and that the game was up.

He went to Ballyduff and turned himself in to Counsellor Robbins, thereby depriving the members of his gang of the opportunity to collect the bounty placed on his head and their chance of obtaining a pardon. In a statement to Counsellor Robbins, he gave a full account of all the robberies he had committed, and the names of his accomplices on each occasion. A number of those named were already in custody on the strength of evidence given by other members of the gang. The remaining few were rounded up and lodged in Kilkenny jail to await trial.

Freney was taken to the barracks in Thomastown, and the next morning was transferred to Kilkenny in a jailer's wagon to face his accusers. During his sojourn in the prison, he was the object of intense curiosity as his reputation was by now countrywide. He had attained the status of living legend. In jail he had to run the gauntlet of several members of his associates' families, as it was their intention to kill him so as to prevent him giving evidence against their kinsmen. However, Freney was never called to the witness box. The thieves convicted one another with conflicting evidence in their attempts to evade the hangman. More than likely his friends in high places, in order to spare him the embarrassment of having to betray his cronies in an open courtroom, used their influence with the bench to proceed with the convictions without his involvement.

Freney's trial took place in Kilkenny city in 1749. He was charged with attempted murder, grand larceny and highway robbery. He was described as a potential murderer, a robber, a traitor, a rapparee, a tory (*toraidhe*) and a rogue of the first degree, and it was recommended that no mercy be extended to him. Several of his former comrades – some awaiting trial and some already convicted and awaiting the gallows – testified against him, turning state evidence in the hope of gaining a reprieve. They were sorely disappointed when no reprieve was forthcoming and no mercy was shown to them. Freney was convicted by the grand jury and sentenced to death by hanging, which was set for five o'clock that same evening.

But Freney escaped the gallows and had the good offices of Lord Carrick to thank, as he intervened on his behalf, requesting that a pardon be granted. In contrast, seven of his gang were executed; only two escaped the death penalty. These two were each given sentences of seven years in jail.

Henry Bushe and Counsellor Robbins were well satisfied with the outcome of the trial. They had succeeded in eliminating the scourge that, for the previous five years, prevented the aristocracy from sleeping easily in their beds without the fear of been robbed.

Lord Carrick's intervention was on condition that Freney depart the country and go to a place of his own choosing, although it's not clear if he ever actually left Ireland. A suggestion that a subscription be collected to defray the expenses of his travel abroad was put before the local gentry, but it fell on deaf ears.

Not only did Carrick save him from the gallows, but he also ensured that he avoided deportation to the New World. It was suggested at the time that the good lord was indebted to the highwayman and was returning a favour. Freney refused to be drawn on the subject as to why the eminent aristocrat intervened on his behalf and saved him from the hangman's noose. The fact that Freney personally knew most of the panel adjudicating on his request for a pardon may have had a favourable influence on his plea for clemency. The overriding consideration in the granting of the pardon was the fact that he never took a human life during his criminal career.

However, not one of his gang succeeded in gaining a pardon, and members of their families felt much aggrieved to see Freney walk away a free man while their loved ones went to the gallows. Any hope they had of a pardon evaporated when Freney surrendered to Counsellor Robbins. If the notorious outlaw had one weakness for a man in his profession, it was his inability to shoot a man dead in cold blood. He recalled that on many occasions, he had had Counsellor Robbins in the sight of his musket but could not bring himself to pull the trigger. Perhaps his Catholic upbringing prevented him from committing the ultimate act that would have consigned him to the history books as a cold-blooded murderer.

Following his pardon, Freney steered clear of crime. Lord Carrick's influence later secured for him the occupation of tidewaiter (customs officer) at the port of New Ross, and Freney was on his best behaviour. Though he had been convicted of serious crimes, he was regarded as a celebrity, and his company was even sought after by members of the gentry.

His repute went beyond his own terrain. In 1754, Freney published his autobiography. Following this, a number of would-be highwaymen from Ennis in County Clare made contact with Freney and suggested that he come and instruct them in the most modern techniques of burglary and highway robbery. They had heard of the little booklet in which he gave an account of his adventures on the highway, and its detailed description of how he and his accomplices had broken into the homes of the gentry and successfully relieved them of their worldly goods. Freney declined this offer in the full knowledge that if he were to cross swords with the law again, a second pardon might not be forthcoming.

A request such as this is an example of the standing the bold Captain had in the minds and hearts of the common people of his day. He had become a legend in his own lifetime and an inspiration to the countless thousands who suffered at the hands of cruel landlords who dished out the most horrendous treatment at will for the least misdemeanour.

Service Rendered

Nicholas Loftus acquired the Mount Eaton estate from John Eaton by a very peculiar and unorthodox method. One night at a party, the two men got involved in a card game. Being under the influence of alcohol, the men allowed the stakes to get out of hand and John Eaton ended up wagering his estate in an effort to recoup the heavy financial loss he had incurred during the night's gambling. His luck deserted him, and he lost his estate.

Next morning, in the cold light of day, he realised his mistake, and tried to renege on the deal made the night before. He was reminded that it was a gentleman's agreement and an honourable outcome was expected of him. Eaton withdrew, saying no way was he going to hand over his estate on account of a gambling debt. At this, Loftus dug in his heels and applied to the sheriff to have Eaton evicted and the estate handed over to him. Eaton enlisted the help of some burly bodyguards to prevent the sheriff from carrying out the eviction, and for well over a year, he thwarted all of Loftus' efforts to gain control of his land. The law of the land was of little use to Loftus, as gambling was frowned upon, and gambling debts were not recognised as legally binding.

Loftus' patience ran out, and he had to consider other means of achieving what he considered to be rightfully his. He was advised to approach James Freney and enlist his aid in removing John Eaton from the estate. Loftus contacted the former highwayman. Having explained his predicament to him, the bold Captain agreed to take up the challenge. Local tradition has no account of how Freney approached this problem or the methods he used to persuade John Eaton to vacate his holdings. But in a short space of time, John Eaton removed himself from the estate and Nicholas Loftus took up residence. Loftus was apparently a very vindictive man, and to obliterate all association of John Eaton with the estate, he renamed it Mount Loftus – the name by which it is still known.

As this was in the early 1750s, Freney had been retired from his highway activities for some years. One must assume that he was handsomely rewarded for his efforts to ensure that John Eaton vacated the estate. There may be some credence to this story as nearly two centuries later, a descendent of Nicholas Loftus, Mrs Grattan-Bellew, presented a blunderbuss to Rothe House in Kilkenny saying it once belonged to the notorious highwayman, the bold 'Captain Freney', and that it was the family's belief that Freney had some connection with Mount Loftus other than the odd time he relieved John Eaton and his family of some of their earthly treasures during the stint he spent as a highwayman.

End of an Era

Freney is said to have died on 20 December, or thereabouts, in the year 1778 at his home at Quay Street, New Ross. He had reached what was considered in those days a very respectable age of sixty-nine years. His family were in very poor circumstances at the time of his death, and were unable to buy a coffin for the once feared highwayman. He was placed in a cart, covered with a blanket and taken home to Inistioge for burial in the family plot by his wife and children. His funeral took place in the midst of a snow storm – an occurrence locals believed was a sure sign that a brave soul had been called home to God. His grave is unmarked, but a plaque on the cemetery wall gives us an approximate location of its whereabouts. Locals believe that it is ten paces down from the boundary wall at the north-western end of the cemetery. Historians today will point out a stone with a horseshoe sculpted on its base which they firmly believe marks the last resting place of the bold Captain and his family.

Even today, the myth and the mystery endure, and the enigma of Freney is compounded by the fact that in Graiguenamanagh, people claim that the once notorious highwayman is buried in St Mullins. The countryside that Freney traversed has changed little over the years. The Nore Valley, Saddle Hill, Brandon Hill and Inistioge village retain their old-world vista and charm, and would be readily recognised by the bold Captain were he to grace these tranquil spots today. Some of his favourite haunts are still much the same as when he frequented them: Freney's Rock, Fossa cemetery [Brownsbarn], Saddle Hill, Brandon Hill, Cullintra Hill, his 'chairs' on the banks of the Barrow, and Brownsford Wood are still to be seen. Even in Ballyduff estate itself, the house that the Freney family lived in is still intact, though now used for storage. It is attached to the coach house on the western boundary of the courtyard, and it is astonishing that it still survives as it is almost three centuries since the bold Captain's family resided there. The folklore of the once notorious highwayman is fast disappearing as conversation and storytelling are replaced by modern methods of communication. His memory is fading like the evening twilight, and may soon be lost in the mists of time.

We can only hope that the spirit of Freney has found its eternal rest, though many believe he still keeps guard over his beloved Nore Valley, where once he held sway.

The Legends Live On

For years after his death, Freney's deeds continued to be recalled. Rumours abounded about the location of his hidden treasure, and even to this day, some people allow themselves the luxury of dreaming of unearthing that elusive pile. Stories have emerged over the years of people from all over Counties Kilkenny and Carlow going out to search on the flimsiest of information in the hope of hitting the jackpot. If some of these stories are to be believed, then a number of fortunate souls have done just that.

The bold Captain lived for nearly thirty years after he quit the highway. We know that his finances at the time of his death were in dire straits so it is hard to imagine that he would have left any booty lying about and not have recovered it. Granted, given the circumstances in which some of it was jettisoned, one can imagine that he had great difficulty trying to locate it. Loot that had been cast into river beds and hidden in the dark of night under extreme pressure may still be lying hidden in the heart of Mother Earth. One can rest assured that very little of it remains unclaimed, and if by chance someone does happen to find some hidden treasure, they can definitely say that they have made a lucky strike. Some of the stories I recounted in this book emerged years after his death, and most certainly will stand in testimony to the impact the bold Captain made during his turbulent lifetime.

Freney the Bold

From New Ross to Castledermot, a scourge he became
The yeomen and gentry recoiled at his name
Travellers they feared the call was for sure
'Stand and Deliver' they had to endure
He robbed from the rich, he gave to the poor
He threatened the mighty from Barrow to Suir
A legend he became in the place he belongs
His name is remembered in story and song.

Taking refuge in the woods, an outcast he became
Hounded by Redcoats enduring hunger and pain
With a price on his head he continued to dare
With his only companion Beefsteaks his mare
No pillow for his head, no bed of his own
He slept on the rocks in the wilds all alone
The lairs and chairs now bearing his name
All landmarks today proclaiming his fame.

Freney the Robber

Their gold and their treasures he took from the rich
He hid them securely in woodland and ditch
Sharing his booty with poor wretches in need
A safe haven to have as he fled from his deeds
He lived by the code that the law was his own
With musket and ball he assaulted their throne
He had many companions but never a friend
They proved their allegiance when it came to the end.

Some sold him out, the gallows to evade
The words traitor and treachery were part of the trade
The ultimate end was surrender and death
Should he sell out his cronies a pardon to get?
He was tried in Kilkenny and sentenced to hang
Lord Carrick reprieved him but none of his gang
A pardon was granted that decided his fate
In order to live he had to emigrate.

The centuries have passed, the legends live on
The days that he spent here, now are long gone
The deeds he accomplished, the courage displayed
Left his foe and adversaries perplexed and dismayed
Calling 'Stand and deliver' from many a hedge
He robbed and he plundered with musket and sledge
He is gone from the scene but the questions abound
If his gold and his treasure still rests in the ground.

by Michael Holden

Freney's Lairs and Hideyholes

Freney's Caves

Several caves in and around Thomastown are said to have been used by the feared outlaw. Local lore tells us that he often sought refuge in a crevice in the rock face that runs parallel to the river at the quay. This crevice was referred to locally as the Monkey Hole. However, its association with the famous highwayman saw it dubbed Freney's Cave. It was an ideal spot for the notorious robber's needs. It can be located today if you walk along the quay and look up towards the convent school – a gaping hole in the cliff face a short distance north-east of the old boys' school facing across the river towards Grennan Castle. As this cave was outside the town wall, it was outside the jurisdiction of the town guardians, and the wanted felon could not be apprehended there.

Dangan Cottage

Another cave used by Freney is in the grounds of Dangan Cottage, and runs parallel to the river into the adjoining property of Dangan Manor. The location of this cave has been lost in the mists of time, but its connection with the famous outlaw reminds us that it once existed.

Dangan Wood

Yet another cave used by Freney is located in Dangan Wood, close to the river, and it was from here that he escaped from the pursuing Redcoats by floating down the Nore at night while clinging to a tree trunk.

The Nore Valley today is a tranquil and peaceful place, and gives little indication of its turbulent past. There is little to remind us of the days when the gentry could not rest easy in their beds for fear of the sound of smashing glass and breaking timber, and the bold Captain announcing his presence at their homes while seeking their most valued possessions.

The Turn Hole

A couple of hundred yards downriver from Dysart Castle, the river takes a fairly sharp turn to the left – forced to divert as it comes into direct contact with the substantial rock foundation that forms the base of Dysart Wood. Over the centuries, the movement of its treacherous currents have eroded the bed of the river at this point, leaving a very deep hole which forms a whirlpool when the river runs high. Freney used to cross the Nore between the castle and this turn. He had years of experience of these treacherous currents, and was well able to negotiate his way around them to the safety of the other side. He was so well acquainted with these treacherous waters that he knew to the nearest yard where he could cross in safety without the drag of the swirling currents sweeping him in the direction of the dangerous turn hole. On many occasions, he used his knowledge of the river to outwit his pursuers by plunging his horse into its waters just above where the currents begin to pull, and then swimming across to the opposite bank. The pursuing soldiers – hoping to shortcut him – plunged their horses into the water just yards above the swirling pool only to be swept headlong into its treacherous hold. Once safely across the river, he had a secret pathway that enabled him and his horse to scale the steep cliff to the safety of Dysart Wood. Local lore tells us that on several occasions, the soldiers were very lucky to escape with their lives, but that their horses paid the price by drowning.

Local stories claim that the bold robber almost lost his life in this whirlpool when he forced his mare to leap into its treacherous waters to avoid being captured. They were swept into the pool, and Freney and Beefsteaks were separated in the churning waters. Both managed to survive and made it onto the rocky edge beneath Dysart Wood. His saddlebags were torn from Beefsteaks' back and swept down into the savage pool, never to be seen again. He divulged later that the bags contained the proceeds of a robbery committed near the Rower, and the lot was lost in his efforts to escape having been sandwiched between two groups of soldiers on the river bank.

The castle and the river valley are much the same today as they were in Freney's time, and if you stroll along the river bank in the late evening, you will feel that sense of history exuding from the scene. You could well imagine the bold Captain in full flight as he evades the pursuing Redcoats across the Nore, gaining the safety of Dysart Wood. Today, local anglers frequent this pool as it has a reputation of playing host to some fine specimen of salmon as they make their way upriver. It is more than likely that Freney also treated himself to a fair share of the silvery delicacy, though he would have taken it from the river using a more clandestine method than present-day fishermen.

Aclare Moat

A fairly substantial mound can be found in the townland of Aclare, which lies midway between Graiguenamanagh and Coppanagh. This mound is likely to be an early Christian burial place, but local history cannot produce any proof to support this theory. Early one morning many years ago, a group of men from Wexford arrived and began to dig into the mound. Local people were naturally disturbed to see an ancient burial place being desecrated, and contacted the parish priest, who put a stop to their gallop, and queried their presence there. A spokesperson for the group told him that they were looking for Freney's buried gold. However, locals are of the opinion that something much more sinister was responsible for their being there that morning, and that they used the pretence of Freney's buried treasure to justify their presence. The group reluctantly withdrew. The excavated earth was never replaced and the mound to this day still bears the scars of that early-morning visit.

Drumroe Castle

A number of people around Mount Loftus firmly believe that Freney buried some of his ill-gotten treasure in the ruin of Drumroe Castle. Others believe that it is in a tunnel that connected the old Eaton House to a ring fort on a nearby hilltop. Another school of thought has it that the treasure hidden in Mount Loftus is from an earlier period, and was placed there by the monks of Duiske Abbey in Graiguenamanagh while on their way to Kilkenny Abbey near Goresbridge as they transferred from one to the other in search of refuge during the period when the abbeys were suppressed in the seventeenth century. Whatever the story, locals believe that the hidden treasure was never recovered, and many around the Mount Loftus estate still harbour dreams of unearthing this hidden hoard. A servant at Mount Loftus in the early years of the nineteenth century was sent to the castle late one night to fetch some wine that was stored in the old ruin. As he was leaving the castle to return to the house, a horse and rider dressed in the quaintest of attire approached from the avenue at great speed, and circled about the ruin three times before vanishing into the gloom, leaving the frightened servant in a state of bewilderment. On returning to the house, he told the master of his experience, and on describing what he had seen was told that it was the ghost of Freney returning to protect his hidden treasure buried in the ruin of the old castle. The master told his servant that if anyone went near the castle at night, Freney and his beloved steed Beefsteaks were on hand to ensure that his treasure remained intact. He admitted to the servant that he had sent him there late that night on purpose, in order to verify the fact that the once notorious highwayman was still on guard in that world beyond ours, and his treasure was still in safe keeping in the ruin of the once beautiful Drumroe Castle.

Coppanagh Gap

If you ascend to the top of Cruchtan Hill, which forms the northern ridge of Coppanagh Gap, and stand in such a position that you can see three counties without turning your head, you are standing on the exact spot where Freney is said to have buried a cache of gold. Counties Kilkenny, Laois and Tipperary can be seen if you stand facing west. If you turn around and move a number of paces across the hilltop, Carlow, Wexford and Waterford come into view, and can all be seen at the same time without turning your head. Which of these viewing points the bold Captain chose to bury his loot is yours for the choosing.

In Freney's time, this hill was used as a lookout where people kept watch for fires on distant hilltops – a signal that others were under siege from the marauding Redcoats and were in need of help. Locals firmly believe in Freney's association with the hill, and some even venture to suggest that the holy-year cross near its top could occupy the site once used by the bold Captain for completely different purposes. Tradition also claims that three other places in which Freney buried caches of gold can be seen from this spot: Brandon Hill, the Blackstairs and Mount Leinster, each of which in its own particular way was associated with Freney.

The Coppanagh hills would have given Freney ample scope to carry out surveillance over the Thomastown, Graiguenamanagh and Gowran area, and would have provided him with plenty of cover to conceal himself from the searching soldiers.

The nearby St Fiachra's well in the adjoining townland of Tickerliven is also reported to have been a favourite resting place of the notorious felon.

Bahana Wood

One evening, as Freney was returning to his den in Bahana Wood, he was surprised by a party of Redcoats. They gave vigorous chase and pursued him into the wood. Owing to the failing light and the canopy of dense foliage, they found it hard to keep sight of him. Freney knew the wood like the back of his hand, and had devised a strategy to help him elude any would-be captors. He led them along a winding path in the direction of the River Barrow, keeping just far enough ahead to allow them fleeting glimpses of him as he approached the river. A mighty oak tree with very low branches grew on a precipice overlooking the river. The Captain, an agile man, had no difficulty in lowering himself down beside his horse, slipping under the low limbs of the tree and jumping his horse down onto the river bank without mishap. The soldiers, not being aware of the danger, rode into the low branches, and ended up in a heap beneath the tree, with their horses crashing over the edge onto the river bank below. This put paid to their chances of capturing the elusive Captain, and proved once again that the crafty robber was equal to the challenge.

Freney's Window in St Mullins

In the ancient ruined monastic settlement of St Mullins, Freney often sought refuge. Here, in this deserted monastic site, you will find a gaping hole high up in the wall of the roofless church. This is known as Freney's Window. The remains of a stone stairway can still be seen protruding from the wall beneath the window, and would have been used by him to ascend to this lofty perch. Although referred to as a window, it is more than likely that this opening in the wall was a doorway that led to a choir gallery or an attic space. It was from here that the bold Captain kept watch for any sign of approaching danger.

The ruins at that time carried a heavy load of ivy that would have given ample cover to anyone who wished to avail of this natural hiding place. St Mullins would have been the ideal retreat for Freney and his like, surrounded as it was by woodlands and set in a secluded valley on the river bank. A constant supply of spring water from St Moling's well and an ample supply of fresh food from the adjoining fields would ensure that he could survive there indefinitely. To this day, several stories are told in the area to this day of the notorious robber and his gang burying treasure in the ruin, in the mound, along the river banks, and in the surrounding woodlands. Some believe that the river bed itself contains loot cast into it in haste while the gang was being hotly pursued by the Redcoats. It is possible that some of this hidden treasure was never retrieved and is still lying there, awaiting the day when the memory of that elusive swashbuckling highwayman known as Freney the Robber will be evoked by someone making a lucky find.

The Devil's Eyebrow

The Devil's Eyebrow is a noted landmark on the bank of the Barrow within sight of Graiguenamanagh. Here, the rock face protrudes from underneath the high ground some thirty to forty feet above the river, and makes a natural vantage point from which to survey the comings and goings over the river near the centre of town. Freney used this natural lookout to his advantage, and on many occasions spied on the Redcoats as they crossed the river in search of his trail. He had the advantage of forewarning and had ample time to retreat to his hideout in Bahana Wood when required. The ruins of Duiske Abbey often offered shelter and succour to the beleaguered Captain. Its many nooks and crannies helped him to avoid capture, as his knowledge of the great ruined abbey gave him a distinct advantage over the pursuing soldiers.

The notorious highwayman was a devout Catholic who had managed to reconcile his Christian beliefs with his criminal activities, even though they more than once brought him into conflict with the local clergy. The clergy themselves were in hiding owing to the penal laws, and had to tend to their flock from the safety of woodland and mountain. In order to avoid the wrath of the authorities, they denounced Freney, claiming that he had tortured a man and threatened to shoot him dead because he suspected him of betraying his whereabouts to the local militia. The priest declared that anyone who offered him sanctuary or shelter would be ostracised from society, and – depending on the circumstances – could even face excommunication. They did so in the hope of avoiding censure by the powers-that-be and to prevent their flock from being harried and hassled by the over-zealous Redcoats. Families in the Inistioge area still recall stories of their great-great-grandparents having suffered greatly owing to some unkindly and unchristian neighbour reporting them to the authorities and claiming they were harbouring the wanted felon. This act of treachery was carried out in the hope of gaining favour with the landlord, and in the expectation of being rewarded with the tenancy of the land from which the unfortunate accused was almost certain to be evicted. Land in those days was a highly emotive issue, and people were prepared to go to any length to acquire it. Even today, the memories of those unpleasant times are often recalled, and country folk can still point out parcels of land from which evictions took place. Freney's own forebears were driven from their land by Cromwell, and even in his own lifetime, the last of the great line of the De Fraynes lost their lands at Brownsford, thus bringing to an end the connection with a once great dynasty that began with the Norman invasion.

Freney's Lair Near Ballyneal

A short distance from Ballyneal Cross is a spot known as Freney's Lair – a low-lying area that held a commanding view over what was at Freney's time the main route from New Ross to Kilkenny. It was in this depression that the bold Captain whiled away many an hour as he waited for some unsuspecting traveller to come along. From this vantage point, he could survey the road before him and would have ample time to prepare himself for an assault on the numerous merchants and gentry who passed by. Merchants in New Ross lost heavily to him, and he was the scourge of the business class, in the Tullogher/Rossbercon/New Ross area, and in south Kilkenny in general. Locals will recall stories they heard from their grandparents about the many times Freney pounced on weary travellers as they returned to New Ross after they had collected payment for goods supplied to merchants in Inistioge and Thomastown. The gentry in and around New Ross did not sleep easy in their beds at night as they were always anticipating a visit from the cursed highwayman. All the area surrounding this local haunt of his has been searched and searched again over the years by hopeful prospectors in pursuit of their ambitions to find Freney's gold. Whether they succeeded or not remains a tight-lipped secret in the area. But many still dream of stumbling on the Captain Freney's gold.

Summerhill Poser

Somewhere in the Summerhill estate, in Kilfane parish, there is a certain spot from where the towers of six castles – the homes of the landed gentry of the day – could be viewed simultaneously. A great number of castles can be seen from the high ground, but to locate the spot from where you see six, and only six, at the same time while looking in one direction is what is referred to as the Summerhill Poser. This is the place Freney chose to bury the fruits of a robbery he committed near Bennettsbridge. Summerhill is an elevated area and has a commanding view of the surrounding countryside of Thomastown, Dungarvan, Tullaherin and Bennettsbridge.

A number of castles could be seen from Summerhill – some still standing and others long gone since Freney's time: the castles of Kilfane, Kilbline, Closhgregg, Stroan, Castlefield (otherwise known as the Black Castle), Bishopslough, Ballinaboula, Castlegarden, Legan, Ballylinch, Clohalla and Neigham. The castles at Stroan and Bishopslough are now demolished, and no trace of them remains. If you could find the spot from where you were once able to see the top of six castles while looking in one direction, you would be standing where Freney supposedly hid his gold. Lots of treasure hunters over the years have tried in vain to pinpoint this exact spot, but difference of opinion regarding the castles in question and the conundrum of seeing six castles together at the same time have made it impossible for anybody to contemplate digging in any particular area.

Local tradition has it that this elusive spot is in the area of the Bluedoor Hill (a blue, timber hunting gate at the entrance to the estate accounts for its name). So, the location of Freney's gold remains as mysterious as ever, and presents a daunting challenge to today's treasure hunters. Hopefully, as time goes on, somebody – perhaps with the help of technology – will succeed where others have failed.

Lochingorra Wood

One of the Captain's favourite hiding places was the wooded area above the river crossing between Dobbinsmill and Kilmacshane, south of the present-day Brownsbarn Bridge. Here was a large area of virgin forest, with which he was well acquainted. Its close proximity to two other woods – Dangan and Dysart (which was then known as Denn's Wood) – gave him added protection on either side of the river, and enabled him to evade pursuing soldiers. Residents of Dobbinsmill today will tell of the existence of a cave that stretched from Lochingorra Wood in the direction of Kilcullen House and in which Freney hid from his pursuers. Once he gained the safety of the wood, he disappeared as if by magic, and no amount of searching ever revealed how or where he concealed himself. Tradition in the area claims that this cave was big enough to allow himself and Beefsteaks to pass through and emerge a considerable distance away out of sight of the searching Redcoats. It is firmly believed around Lochingorra today that some of his plundered gains still remain hidden in that cave. However, he never divulged its whereabouts to anyone. Sceptics claim it never existed, but the many times he managed to vanish from the face of the earth after entering Lochingorra Wood definitely suggests he had some means of concealment that remained undetected. The presence of such a cave is the most likely answer to this riddle.

Over the centuries, treasure hunters have searched for the cave, but it seems as elusive as much of Freney's gold, and today no one is sure that it ever existed. The many miraculous disappearances of the bold Captain in this wood would seem to give credence to the existence of some type of outlet, such as the supposed cave, that allowed him evade his constant pursuers.

Today, the wood is a very different place from the days the brave highwayman lived out his precarious lifestyle in its verdant surrounds. The tranquillity and peace of it today give little hint of its turbulent past, but surely this is the one spot where the spirit of the notorious Captain astride his beloved Beefsteaks would roam the land at night. Walking in Lochingorra Wood today, you can feel that sense of history and there is an air of expectancy that the bold Captain might appear around the next turn.

The Blindman's Window

Where the Rock Road at Dysart overhangs the River Nore, a mile due south of Thomastown as you travel towards Ballyduff, was where Freney had one of his most secure hiding places. Here, the rock face rises sharply up from the water's edge and ascends steeply to a height of approximately one hundred feet. High up on this craggy cliff face was a natural cave that ran some twenty feet into the interior of the rock. The entrance was concealed by a section of flag that protruded upwards, blinding off the cavity and shielding it from the attention of those who travelled the river bank below. This secure retreat was a short distance from his lookout, the rock on the high ground at Carrickmourne. From here, he had a commanding view of the Nore Valley, and was able to monitor the movements of the Redcoats as they made excursions between Thomastown and Inistioge along the river bank. Having caught sight of them, he could scurry across the river to the safety of this hideout and lie low until the danger had passed.

Access to this cave was made easier during the Great Famine, when the Board of Guardians in Thomastown decided to build a new road from Grennan to Ballyduff so as to give employment to the starving locals. This new road was hewn out of the rock face midway up the cliff, thus leaving what was Freney's former hideout exposed just above the present road. As a result of these excavations, several boulders that formed the roof collapsed, and the cave was almost obliterated. The indent in the cliff face that remains is still referred to as The Blindman's Window. Unfortunately, the name has almost disappeared from local history, and very few people know of its exact location today. Local lore enthusiasts described it as the perfect hiding place. From behind the protruding crag that concealed the opening, Freney had a perfect view up and down the river bank. The name Blindman's Window more than likely originated from the fact that Freney had lost the sight of one eye after suffering a bout of smallpox.

The passage of time has taken its toll on the once secure hideout, but the memory of the man that it once paid host to connects us today to a period when highwaymen roamed the land. The workforce who laboured on the construction of this road probably never realised that life-and-death situations were played out in the vicinity of the cave, or the important role it played in the adventures of our most famous highwayman, Freney the Robber.

Treasure at the Kerry-hole

Along the banks of the Clodiagh stream from the New Ross road to the River Nore, was an area where Freney spent a lot of his leisure time. The source of the Clodiagh stream is on the south-western slopes of Brandon Hill and follows the gentle incline in the direction of the river. This little tributary joins the Nore at what is known as the Kerry-hole or Kerry-ford. As the stream approaches the river, it makes a rapid descent through a densely wooded area and over steep, rocky crags that at one point causes it to develop into a sizeable waterfall. You can hear the sound of the cascading waters as they approach the river junction. Local tradition asserts that the pool formed under the waterfall is a bottomless hole, and a place best avoided. Fishermen and river travellers swore that a supernatural presence could be sensed at this spot, and some locals believed it to be the mouth of Hell. In Freney's day this whole area was covered in dense forest and made an ideal hiding place for the bold highwayman and his gang. Local stories claim that he buried a cache of gold along with his blunderbuss among the crags in the bed of the stream close to this waterfall.

Over a century and a half after Freney's death, a local man found the remains of an old gun in the river bed, and word of this find started a flurry of treasure hunting by people who believed that Freney's gold was about to be revealed. Nothing more was found, but locals were convinced that the man who uncovered the relic on that occasion did not confess to all his luck.

The old belief held locally that this pool was bottomless was put to the test shortly after the Famine. An attempt was made to verify this claim by locals who tied two half-hundredweights together, attached them to several lengths of rope, and lowered them into its depths. They descended rapidly until all the rope was used up. Then lengths of binding twine were added and they continued to feed it into the murky waters. The twine – unable to take the strain – snapped, letting the lot disappear into the depths below. This definitely convinced those present that the Kerry-hole was indeed a bottomless pit. Shortly afterwards, a local youth who had emigrated to Australia wrote home to report that he had found the two half-hundredweights tied together with rope attached to a length of twine on a beach between Sydney and Newcastle as he went for a morning stroll. This snippet of information may have convinced the locals that the Kerry-hole was indeed a shortcut to Australia.

Brownsford Wood and Freney's Chair

A short distance from the cross of Ballyneal, you will find another of his hideouts known locally as Freney's Chair. It was here in Brownsford Wood that he took refuge when the going got tough. The chair – a formation in a rock face jutting out in the highest point of the wood – allowed him overall surveillance of the valley below. A natural conformation, it allowed him to sit back and relax at will. He used a shallow crevice in its side to cradle his blunderbuss, and a small, flat ledge jutting out at the other side he used as a table. This rock is still visible today, and serves as a permanent reminder of the turbulent past that was part and parcel of the history of this wood.

Freney is believed to have buried much of his treasure in this wood, and locals will tell you of treasure hunters coming out from New Ross and searching the wood hoping to come upon the elusive pile. A story is told in the area of a forebear of the bold Captain – a man known as the Knight De Frayne – burying a tailor alive by standing the man upright in a field because he had not completed a suit of clothes for him on time. He is said to have buried the tailor in what was then rough ground, and put a pile of rocks on top of the grave to conceal his dastardly deed. The tailor is said to have cursed the knight as he was being lowered into the hole, saying that the day will come when generations of the name De Frayne will pay dearly for this barbaric act and his untimely end. Local tradition claims that this curse was responsible for the De Frayne family losing all its possessions in Ballyreddy and Brownsford. Locals can still point out the spot referred to as the 'grave in the field' which has since been reclaimed and is now arable land. A local tenant farmer many years ago decided to reclaim this patch to sow wheat. While the work was in progress, he decided to remove the stone cairn that marked the spot reputed to be the tailor's grave, believing that the story was an old wives' tale. On removing some of the stones, an upright skeleton was found along with some items of a tailor's trade: a rusty scissors and thimble. The workforce withdrew in fear as they realised that the story of the tailor's demise could in fact be true. They firmly believed that anybody who interfered with a burial site would be dogged by bad luck for the remainder of their life.

Historians in the area also claim that a number of disused cemeteries nearby were used by the bold robber to conceal his ill-gotten gains. More than likely, they witnessed the same activity as the above mentioned places, with the night air echoing to the sound of picks and shovels being worked strenuously in the hope of unearthing sudden riches.

New Ross Women Visit Dranagh

In a field in the townland of Dranagh, which lies between St Mullins and Glynn, you can still see the result of the efforts of a group of ladies from New Ross who descended on the area in the hope of unearthing some of Freney's hidden gold. Word around New Ross was that the bold Captain had buried the takings of a night's plundering in the corner of this secluded field. This was rough ground and not very accessible from the nearby road. The owner of the land in question was of the belief that the spot where the first rays of the rising sun over the Blackstairs would be touched by the last rays of the setting sun over Brandon was where Freney chose to bury his gold. After monitoring both the sunrise and sunset, the women began to dig at a chosen spot. After spending several hours of intense and laborious digging, the enthusiasm of the New Ross ladies for treasure hunting waned and they returned home with nothing to show for all their efforts but blistered fingers. They dug up an area of some twenty square yards, and the outline of this activity could still be seen up to recent times. It is said in the area that they returned on several occasions, but were never lucky enough to unearth any of the highwayman's elusive treasure.

Dysart Wood and The Famine Road

In order to give some relief to the starving locals in the years after the Famine, the Board of Guardians in Thomastown

decided to construct a roadway through the upper part of
Dysart Wood. This would have been a continuation of what
we now know as the Rock Road. Many people were employed
at this work, which was very laborious as everything had to be
done by physical effort. It consisted of removing obstructions
such as boulders, trees and anything else that lay in the path of
the road to one side. One evening, two brothers were heaving
a heavy rock with a crowbar when they heard what sounded
like crunching glass. On moving the rock to one side, they
saw a broken slate, and on removing it found the remains of a
crushed earthenware jar underneath, its fragments mixed with
a selection of gold coins. They covered it over with clay so none
of the other workers would become aware of its presence. They
watched over it carefully until everyone had gone home that
evening. Later that night, they returned and dug up their find.
As they were putting the coins in a bag, they were attacked by
a ferocious dog and were lucky to make their escape with their
bag of coins intact. Residents of Dysart will tell you that a large
black dog was known to patrol the area of the wood around
St Coleman's well at night. This dog was believed to be the
spirit of a man who was the bane of the saint's life during the
time he spent here. To atone for his wrongdoings, this man's
spirit was condemned to roam the wood, where he inflicted so
much torment on the hermit saint during his lifetime. Whether
this was the same dog that attacked the brothers, we will never
know, but if it was, it apparently failed in its attempt to prevent
them from getting their hands on the hidden gold. Shortly

afterwards the two brothers set sail for America from the port of New Ross, possibly on the *Dunbrody*. The Famine road was never completed, and the remains of this effort can still be seen in Dysart Wood today. The gold the brothers found was attributed to Freney and his gang. The legend of Freney having hidden gold in both Dysart Wood still persists in the area and the cemetery attached to Dysart Castle, the one-time home of the famous Bishop Berkeley, who was born in 1685. This connection leads to a very interesting history of the castle and its hinterland. The Berkeley family had vacated the area around the time that Freney commenced his highway activities, and it is quite possible that the castle was by then lying vacant and was used by Freney as a country retreat and a place of refuge.

Ballycocksouis Gives Up its Gold

Shortly after the Famine, at harvest time, a farmer named Hogan who lived in Ballycocksouis, was bringing home stones to construct the base of a threshing stack. It was the custom at that time for farmers to enlist the help of young men from the workhouse during the busy time of the year, to help with harvesting and haymaking. Such was the case with Mr Hogan. Working with a teenager, he began collecting stones from a wall on the farm to take into the haggard so as to construct a stone base on which the sheaves of corn would be stacked to await threshing. As they removed the stones, a jingling sound was heard within the crumbling wall. The youth remarked on this to Mr Hogan, enquiring what might have caused the sound. The wily old farmer recognised the noise but pretended to have heard nothing. He then instructed the youth to return to the farmyard and let loose a horse to graze that he had forgotten to release before they came out. The youth went in the direction of the yard, but cut back by the other side of the ditch to a spot where he could see his employer. Here, he watched as the farmer withdrew his hand from the wall, scrutinised what it contained, and then deposited the items into his pocket. This he repeated several times while looking around to see if anybody was observing him.

The young teenager then went and let out the horse and returned to his employer's side. He again asked his boss what might have made the jingling noise, only to be told that it was probably shingle falling through the stones as they removed them. The youth was not convinced, but said nothing. That night in the local public house, he told his neighbours about what had happened that day, and that he suspected Mr Hogan had played cute and had pocketed a find of some description. Not long after, the youth's suspicions were proved correct as Hogan built a new house. He purchased adjoining land and increased his stock numbers. The neighbours were convinced that Freney's gold contributed to the welfare of the Hogan farmstead. This story survives to the present day, and is still told around the firesides on the high ground between Inistioge and Ballyhale.

Missed Meeting at the Knockrue

A widow woman who lived near Killarney, in Thomastown parish, had strong republican leanings and allowed her home to be used as a safe house by the IRA. She later recounted a story she heard from a member who called to her one night for food and shelter. After eating a meal and indulging in a few mugs of porter, he let slip a story about two members who were on the run and were hiding out in the Knockrue, a wood on the Mount Juliet estate. A comrade and himself had arranged to meet them at the highest point, that being the part of the wood over-looking Killarney.

Having arrived at the agreed time and after waiting for a considerable period, the two men on the run failed to show. The others, being concerned for their safety, began to look for them. After failing to get a response to their coded system of communication – the curlew's call – they began searching the usual haunts frequented in the wood by men on the run, but no sign of them could be found. They were taking a short cut back to their hideout when they came across a bank of earth that showed signs of having been freshly dug out.

On closer investigation, they found the remains of a very decayed and rusted musket, and immediately suspected that someone had hit upon buried treasure. Some years later, after the troubles in the country had quietened down, one of the two who had failed to make the meeting at the Knockrue bought a substantial farm, and it was suggested that Freney's gold was a major contributor to this venture.

Timber Felling in Lochingorra Wood

In the 1940s, a logging firm – Hearne's of Waterford – moved in to Lochingorra Wood to fell its mature timber. Several local people were employed by this company, and they were well aware of the connection Freney had with this wood. As soon as they moved into the wood, all their thoughts were on Freney's gold. They were certain that before the job was over, a lucky strike was bound to happen. The tallest tree in the forest – a mighty oak – was believed to contain some of the bold Captain's buried loot beneath its roots. From a vantage point on the high ground near Prendergast's house in Kilmacshane, this tree was clearly visible as its lofty crown swayed high above the rest of the forest. The workforce lost no time in establishing its exact location, and lived for the day when it was next in line for felling. Only then could they pry among its roots to try to find what they hoped was lying underneath. Eventually, they felled the forest giant and put in three days of back-breaking and laborious digging as they excavated the base and roots in anticipation of a fruitful return for their efforts. Unfortunately for them, the king of the forest failed to reveal its secrets. When the tree was taken to the sawmill for planking, several lead balls were found embedded deep in its trunk, leading people to conclude that they were possibly there since the notorious robber sought its shelter. Lochingorra failed to give up its secrets to the eager timber loggers, and the search goes on. The myth and the legend remain intact, and only if someone unearths the hidden hoard in the future, will the ghosts be put to rest.

Gold Fever in Goresbridge

On the western outskirts of the village of Goresbridge lies the townland of Lowergrange. Here in the marshy ground on the bank of a tiny tributary of the Barrow can be found a mighty spring well. A grotto dedicated to the Virgin Mary was erected beside the well in the holy year of 1950, and can be seen from the road as you approach the village from Gowran. Early in the twentieth century, a group of men were clearing drains beside this well. Each man was assigned a certain section of drain to clear, and the work progressed favourably for a few days. One morning, one of the workmen failed to report for work, and when enquiries were made as to why he was absent, the reply was that he was going to America. This surprised the others, but the reason for it became apparent the next day when another man put to work on the drain in his place discovered a flagstone in the side of the drain that appeared to have been prized loose. On removing it, a small cavity was discovered behind it, which showed all the hallmarks of having contained some hidden objects. The men pondered the discovery, and one of them remembered that the man in question did not go to his dinner the day before but remained behind, saying that his stomach was unsettled and he had no appetite. The men concluded that he had come upon buried treasure, and the amount must have been pretty substantial if it necessitated his emigrating in order to protect his find.

Immediately, speculation ran wild in the area, for it was believed locally that Freney the Robber had buried the proceeds of a nearby robbery in this very bog, and it was likely that this man had unearthed it. However, speculation being speculation, the truth will never be known, but the story persists to this day, and people in Goresbridge still readily recall it.

Freney's Autobiography

James Freney wrote his autobiography – *Life and Times of James Freney* – in 1754, but confined it to the short number of years he engaged in his highway activity. He tells us little of his early life, and omits mention of the deeds that laid the foundations for the stories of magic, myth and mystery that grew around him and which ensured his place in the history books. It is said that he was a very modest man who avoided publicity and who never made any reference to his many acts of kindness, either during his highway career or over the remainder of his life. It is possible that by keeping silent or by playing down the existence of these acts of kindness, he fostered an image of a heartless ruffian who showed no mercy and was a person not to be crossed.

Nothing is known of his life for the twenty years after his autobiography was published, but records show that he was employed by the New Ross Harbour Board as a tide waiter in 1776. This appointment was surely a classic example of 'hiring a thief to catch a thief', as the job involved locating contraband being smuggled into the port of New Ross on board the many schooners that plied their trade in and out of Ireland at that time. How long a period he was employed by the Harbour Board is not known, but it appears that his friends in high places continued to support him long after he retired from the highway.

Many people are sceptical as to whether or not Freney penned his own autobiography. It is suggested that he enlisted the help of a ghost writer, as he was not educated enough and did not have the ability to accomplish this task himself. However, I beg to differ. His autobiography informs us that he attended school for seven years, and benefited from private tuition paid for by the matriarch of Ballyduff House, old Mrs Robbins. I am firmly convinced that his association with some of the most educated people in the land – namely Counsellor Robbins and his associates, who came to Ballyduff on regular visits – must also have been of some benefit to him. Surely some of their literary and linguistic expertise would have rubbed off, enabling him to acquire the ability to accomplish this task. He was regarded as a brilliant conversationalist who possessed a sharp wit and a beguiling sense of humour. I believe that he is indeed the author of the *Life and Times of James Freney*. Although he was fluent in Irish, his autobiography was penned in English – probably because the English-speaking members of the population were the only ones who would have been able to afford to buy it. It was reprinted several times, and at one stage was included as part of the curriculum in many hedge schools around the country. Apparently, his need for money was responsible for this effort, and as Dr Johnson once said, only a blockhead would write for any other reason than money. He dedicated his autobiography to the man he owed his life to, Lord Carrick. The following is the text of a letter to that effect:

To the right honourable Somerset Hamilton Butler, Earl of Carrick.

My Lord, as I owe my life to your Lordship, by whose interest and intercession I obtained his Majesty's pardon, I am in duty bound to dedicate the following account of my past life to your Lordship; and your own well known zeal to serve your country, for which the grand jury of the county of Kilkenny, in the most public manner, at the close of their presentments, returned to you, on behalf of the county, their most sincere thanks, entitle you to a preference, before all others, to the patronage of this account of my past life, in which I have avoided as much as I could enlarging on the pains and expenses your Lordship was at in abolishing that notion and scheme of protection which had for too many years prevailed in the county of Kilkenny, and was the real source from whence the practice of horse, cow and sheep stealing and house-breaking sprang, and continued so long in that county; for, the many honest and well-meaning men, either through indolence or backwardness, suffer a few who regard only their own profit, and not the welfare of their neighbours, or the public, to make use of indirect means to screen and save the guilty, your Lordship's zeal and resolution has roused up others to imitate your example, and to concur in preventing such pernicious schemes from taking effect as formerly. This is a truth so well known and allowed of, that anything I could say to prove it might look ridiculous, and I fear, offend your Lordship, who chose to do good merely for the sake of doing good, without any notion or desire of ostentation or being rewarded on that account; both of which I am sensible you have too great a soul not to despise. I shall pray for the welfare and happiness of your Lordship and your family, who am your Lordship's most humble servant.

James Freney

Knight of the Road

In the year 1890, Percy French, the noted songwriter and composer, put together a comic sketch entitled *Knight of the Road* based on the adventures of the bold Captain Freney. It was a comic opera and was first presented in the Queen's Royal Theatre in Dublin in April 1891. This was a completely new approach to opera, where comedy was introduced into what had hitherto been a very serious side of the musical world. Exposure such as this brought new fame to Freney over a hundred years after his departure from this world. Percy French had a magical way of integrating comedy and reality, and Freney's exploits gave him a golden opportunity to combine both, and bring to the stage the story of one of the most daring desperadoes of the previous century.

The opera was well received in Dublin, and catapulted the bold Captain yet again onto the public scene. His book became a much-sought-after item, and was introduced to the school curriculum of the day. Students must have relived some of his more daring escapades in their daydreams as their teachers took them through its exciting pages.

Had the bold highwayman been alive in Percy French's time, he would surely have been miffed to find himself the subject of comic opera for the enjoyment of the nobility of the land. One wonders if his fickle sense of humour would have tolerated this exposure, and one can well imagine that it was in Percy's best interest that the notorious Captain was long gone from the scene.

Come All Ye Fine Ladies
(from *Knight of the Road*)

Come all ye fine ladies and gentlemen, too
Attend to me singing and I'll tell you true
About a brave lad who lived out in the cold
And the name that he went by was Freney the bold.

Chorus
Freney the bold, turinah, turinah, turinan the danday.

Now James was a robber upon the highway
He stopped the stage coaches by night and by day
What he took from the rich he gave to the poor
So of poverty's blessing he always was sure.

Chorus

One day when the coach had set off for the fair
It was met by James Freney bestriding his mare
Some called for the soldiers, some called for the watch
And one old lady called for twopence worth of scotch.

Chorus

The guard held his blunderbuss out at full cock
Sez he, 'James, clear out, or you'll know what's o'clock'
James flattened him out with the butt of his gun
Sez he, 'What's o'clock well, it's just striking one.'

Chorus

So the gentlemen pulled out their purses of gold
And handed them over to Freney the bold
Sez Freney, 'Me boys, ye got off mighty well
I'd have fleeced you far more if I'd kept a hotel.'

Chorus

Now all ye fine ladies and gentlemen, too
Ye've heard from my singing, and I'd told ye true
All about the brave boy who lived out in the cold
And the name that he went by was Freney the bold.

The Trial of James Freney

The following paper concerning the trial of Freney and his gang was submitted to a meeting of the Royal Society of Antiquaries of Ireland by Mr J. G. Prim around 1849. It includes a letter written by William Colles to Francis Bindon in which an account is given of the trial of Freney's gang in Kilkenny and the executions.

This article contributed by Mr J. G. Prim to the Society illustrates the state of society in Kilkenny at this time. The following letter, written in the middle of the last century [1849], may, I think, fairly claim to be preserved, by being placed on record in the Society's proceedings, as it serves to illustrate the state of society in Kilkenny at that period, when the system of secretly countenancing and protecting highwaymen was pretty general amongst the better classes throughout all parts of Great Britain and Ireland, but seems to have prevailed to so much larger an extent in the county of Kilkenny as to cast a particular strain upon the character of the district. Towards the close of the previous century, the government itself set a bad example in this respect, by granting 'protections' to notorious robbers, for service to be performed in the way of apprehending and delivering up to justice, or giving such information as would enable the authorities to capture other depredators, frequently their own associates in crime; and thus 'set a thief to catch a thief'. The grand jury of the county of Kilkenny appear to have acted on this proverb, when in the year 1686–7, they 'presented' the propriety of taking into the King's protection the leader of a gang of Tories, or outlaws, then infesting the county, as the best course to suppress robberies and felonies in and about this part of the Kingdome, and when those desperadoes were not alone pardoned their own offences, but were allowed the use of 'their horses and travelling defensive arms' whilst engaged in the service of the state for the suppression of other criminals. This system seems to have continued for many years subsequently; and where the government of the country, and those charged with the administration of the laws, were to be found entering into compromises and compacts with the most notorious offenders, it can scarcely be wondered at if individuals, even of a superior class of society, should have been occasionally found ready to screen or harbour the outlaw, to insure his assistance against other robbers, in a most unsettled time when the state was totally unable to protect the subject from such visitations. Such an effect ought to have been expected as the natural consequence of the system; and James Freney, the celebrated highwayman of the last century, to whom reference is made in the letter to which I now direct attention, has borne evidence to the fact, that the arrangement of permitting protections to be given to robbers was the cause of all the crime which was so rife in Kilkenny and the surrounding counties at the period when he flourished and bequeathed to literature his *Life and Adventures*. It would seem that, at the time when the letter was written, the nobility and principal gentry of the county had resolved to make a determined effort to put down highwaymen and their protectors, and in that effort they eventually succeeded, although the agency through which it was effected was still that of pardoning and patronising the principal rogue, on the condition of his aiding to convict his accomplices. The letter was written by Alderman William Colles, the originator of the trade in Kilkenny marble, and inventor of the ingenious machinery by which the cutting and polishing of the stone is carried out. It is addressed to Francis Bindon, of Limerick, an eminent architect of the day, from whose designs the mansions of Woodstock and Bessborough were erected. Mr Colles had been the contractor for the building. I am indebted for a copy of the document to the great grandson of that gentleman, Mr Alexander Colles of Millmount.

To Francis Bindon, esq., at Ennis.
Kilkenny, August 13th 1749.

D' sir, I this moment received your letter of the 11th,
and as our assizes ended last night I shall give you as
circumstantial an acc' of what was done at them as I
can. On Monday the Grand Jury was sworn. On the
panel of which the High Sheriff took care to put none
but Gentlemen of y' best ffortunes and characters in y'
county; S.W. Ffowns was foreman. One Corrigan who
got his pardon last assizes for prosecuting Stotesbury
was found guilty of horse stealing: as also James Bulger
and another proclaimed man known by y' name of
Bristeen were arraigned on the proclamation and being
convicted of being y' same persons were executed that
afternoon at 5 o'clock, and Bulger was on Thursday
hanged in chains on y' road to Callan where Burgess
was shot. On Wednesday, Stack was convicted of
robbery and Martin Millea a man of substance was
found guilty of harbouring Jaffreney, on full evidence,
as was on Thursday one Larresy for y' same crime, and
two others, not proclaimed, for robberys, besides 4 or
5 small offences. So that we have eight under sentence
who are all to be executed on Saturday next, Stotesbury
appeared and pleaded his pardon; and was given security
to material evidence ag' harbourers; the most part of y'
gentlemen of y' county gave undeniable proofs of their
hearty endeavours to retrieve this county from the

scandalous imputation it lay under, as if the bulk of y'
county were favourers of the rogues; and those few ag'
whom any imputation of that King lay were greatly
discountenanced by the rest but nothing could be so
far fixed on any particular person as to bring them to
public trial. The assizes ended last night with the Grand
Jury's both of the county and the city returning Lord
Carrick public thanks, for his activity, care, and vigour
in suppressing this gang of rogues which appeared to
be much more numerous than was supposed; four more
who were formerly unknown being presented by y'
Grand Jury in order to be proclaimed.

'Y' most obed' humble serv', W. Colles.

As I have already alluded to the highwayman Freney,
and have quoted so largely from his *Life and Adventures*
in the notes which I have appended to the foregoing
letter, perhaps I may be permitted, by way of appendix
to the document, to mention a few further particulars
about that notorious personage. Freney, although usually
enumerated amongst the 'gentlemen robbers' who
achieved an unenviable reputation in the last century,
was, in reality, of humble birth, his father having been
the confidential servant of Joseph Robbins, Esq., of
Ballyduffe, whom he faithfully served; the son also acted
in a menial capacity in the employment of the Robbins
family, until he became dissipated, and took to the road.

He was, however, most probably, descended from one of the first Anglo-Norman families in the country – the De La Fraynes, of Ballyreddy, who, having long held a leading position, and for centuries, almost without intermission, filled the important office of seneschal of the liberty of Kilkenny, by forfeiture of property for their political attachments, ultimately descended, in some branches of the race, to the lowest rank. But with the predatory predilections of the old feudal chieftains, Captain Freney, as he was called, also inherited much of the chivalrous feeling of his knightly ancestors, and his name has been handed down to us as a most daring and successful freebooter, but unstained by any act of revolting atrocity. He was particularly gallant towards the ladies whom he encountered in his professional excursions, and a woman had no fear of being robbed by him; whilst even in his treatment of the other sex, he frequently behaved with much forbearance, and even generosity, always sparing the purse of the poor man, and most scrupulously returning to the wealthy person whom he had 'delivered' a sum sufficient to bear his expenses to his journey's end. His exploits on the highway are not only chronicled in his own curious autobiography, but are preserved in the traditions of the peasantry, and have been read, recounted, and sung throughout Ireland. I would here beg leave to introduce to the members of the society one of the rude contemporary ballads of which his adventures formed the theme. I often heard it recited by an aged female relative, who remembered frequently to have seen, and even conversed with the 'bold Captain Freney' in her youth; and I recently was fortunate enough to obtain the words from an old servant of hers, from whose lips, also, Mr William Ranslow, organist of St Chanice's Cathedral, kindly noted down the air, for the purpose of its preservation in the Society's proceedings. I may remark that, although this old ballad is now almost forgotten in the county of Kilkenny, where no doubt, it was originally composed, it may be found amongst the peasantry in other districts. A Kilkenny friend of mine, whilst exploring the matchless scenery of the Lakes of Killarney, about two years since, was no less surprised than interested at hearing his boatman, amongst other songs, sing in full chorus that of:

Bold Captain Freney

One morning as I being free from care
I rode abroad to take the air
'Twas my fortune for to spy
A jolly Quaker riding by.

Chorus

And it's oh, bold Captain Freney!
Oh bold Freney, oh.

Said the Quaker – I'm very glad
That I have met with such a lad
There is a robber on the way
Bold Captain Freney, I hear them say.

Chorus

Captain Freney I disregard
Although about me I carry my charge
Because I being so cunning and cute
It's where I hide it's within my boot.

Chorus

Says the Quaker: It is a friend
His secret unto me would lend
I'll tell you where my gold does lie
I have it sewed beneath my thigh.

Chorus

As we rode down to Thomastown
Bold Freney bid me to light down
Kind sir, your breeches you must resign
Come, quick, strip off, and put on mine.

Chorus

Says the Quaker: I do not think
That you'd play me such a roguish trick
As my breeches I must resign
I think you are no friend of mine.

Chorus

As we rode a little on the way
We met a tailor dressed most gay
I boldly bid him for to stand
Thinking he was some gentleman.

Chorus

Upon his pocket I laid hold
The first thing I got was a purse of gold
The next thing I found, which me surprised
Was a needle, a thimble, and chalk likewise.

Chorus

Your dirty trifle I disdain
With that I return'd him his gold again
I'll rob no tailor if I can
I'd rather ten times rob a man.

Chorus

It's time for me to look about
There's a proclamation just gone out

There's fifty pounds bid on my head
To bring me in, alive or dead.

Chorus

Little History of
Mount Juliet Estate

This part of Ireland has very strong Norman associations, particularly with the great Butler family, who have played a prominent part in the history of Mount Juliet.

The estate as we know it today was originally two separate estates, Walton's Grove and Ballylinch, each with its own distinct history.

Walton's Grove

The Waltons were an ancient Norman family who owned Oldtown, the townland of Mount Juliet. They changed the name Oldtown to Walton's Grove. They were here for centuries, until Cromwell dispossessed William Walton in 1653. An unknown Cromwellian owned Walton's Grove for a short period, but after the Restoration it became the property of James, Duke of York, later James II. James sold it to a Mr Sweet, who in turn sold it to Mr Kendall in 1719. He changed the name to Kendall's Grove.

One stormy winter's night, 'old Mr Kendall' as he was known, was robbed by highwaymen and an important portfolio was taken. He begged the Reverend Thomas Burke to retrieve it for him. Reverend Burke duly caught the robbers and returned the portfolio. Old Mr Kendall was so overcome with gratitude that he left all his property, including Kendall's Grove, to Reverend Burke. Unfortunately, Burke was wildly extravagant and had to sell all his property to settle his debts. He sold Kendall's Grove in 1757 to his neighbour, the Earl of Carrick, who built Mount Juliet on this land.

Ballylinch

This part of the estate is now a thriving stud farm and an integral part of day-to-day life on the estate. It was originally called Bally Inch, which is a translation of the Gaelic *Baile Inse*, meaning the peninsulated townland.

The townlands and castles of Legan and Ballylinch belonged to Jerpoint Abbey until the Suppression of the Monasteries by Henry VIII in 1541. They were then granted to Thomas, Earl of Ormonde (the Black Earl), who in turn granted them to Oliver Grace, a descendant of the Norman adventurer Raymond Fitzwilliam le Gros.

Oliver's son Gerald built Ballylinch Castle and moved here from Legan Castle in 1563. However, Cromwell granted Ballylinch to one of his followers, Colonel Daniel Redman, in 1654, dispossessing the Graces. Redman's daughter Eleanor married James Butler, 3rd Viscount Ikerrin, and the Butlers of Ikerrin moved their residence to Ballylinch from Lismalin in Tipperary.

In 1757 the Reverend Thomas Burke sold what had formerly been Walton's Grove to his neighbour, Somerset Hamilton Butler, 8th Viscount Ikerrin, 1st Earl of Carrick, thus amalgamating the two estates.

The Earl of Carrick built a new mansion on the banks of the River Nore and called it Mount Juliet in tribute to his wife, Lady Juliana, always known as Juliet. The family moved from Ballylinch Castle, which was mostly torn down, to Mount Juliet and remained there until 1914, when they sold the estate to the McCalmont family who lived there until recently.

Acknowledgements

My grateful thanks to the people listed here and to whom I owe a very deep debt of gratitude for the help, encouragement and assistance they willingly gave me in so many ways when putting these stories together.

I thank my family for putting up with the inconvenience over the past three years, as I collected and researched these stories, and whose computer skills enabled me to get this far. I cannot thank enough Joe Doyle, my colleague in Dúchas, for his interest, encouragement, support and time so willingly given as I endeavoured to compile this book.

I salute most gratefully many other people, especially those who have passed to their eternal reward; their stories will live on and their names will be remembered, at least in the leaves of this book: Danny Brady, Fidawn, Inistioge; Dan Brennan, Ballygub, Inistioge; Eddie Cody, High Street, Inistioge; Frank Clarke, Glynn, St Mullins; Caroline and Seamus Corballis, Castlefield House, Dungarvan; Eddie Doran, Tinnahinch, Graiguenamanagh; Dixie Doyle, Carrickmourne, Thomastown; Joseph Doyle, Smithstown, Thomastown; Frank

Delahunty, Smithstown, Thomastown; Pat Dunphy, Centra, Thomastown; Dúchas, Heritage Society, Tullaherin; Michael Furlong, Tickerliven, Graiguenamanagh; Willie Grace, Dysart, Thomastown; Micéal Hanrahan, Tullogher, New Ross; Lena Holden, Dysart, Thomastown; James Holden, Castlegarden, Thomastown; Willie Holden, Mill Road, Inistioge; James Holden, Dysart, Thomastown; Peter Kealy, Dranagh, St Mullins; Jack Kelly, Mounteenmore, Dungarvan; Nelly Kelly, Rosboultra, Ballyhale; Edward Law, Bishopslough, Bennettsbridge; Denis Lee, Mill Road, Inistioge; John Masterson, Stroan, Thomastown; Dick McElwee, Ballyknock, New Ross; Bernie Mahon, Goersbridge; Tabo Morrissey, Stoneen, Thomastown; Danny McDonald, Rockview, Inistioge; Johnny McGrath, Kilmanaheen, Dungarvan; Mick Murphy, Kilfane, Thomastown; Moses Murphy, St Mullins; Mick O'Neill, Cappagh, Inistioge; John O'Sullivan, Knockbrack, Thomastown; Jim Power, Smithstown, Thomastown; Rothe House, Kilkenny; Royal Society of Antiquaries of Ireland; Donie Sherdian, Ennisnag Lounge; Peter Sommerville-Large, Ullard, Borris; Brede Thomas, Ballyduff House, Thomastown; James Wallace, Stonecarthy, Stoneyford; Walter Walsh, Stoneen, Thomastown.

I salute most heartily the men and women named above. I appreciate their generosity and open-handedness in willingly giving of their time and in sharing their stories of the bold Captain with me. I hope that by committing these stories to paper, I have done some service to our area in preserving for posterity the folklore and heritage of a long-forgotten age.

Author Profile

Michael Holden, who lives in Castlegarden, Thomastown, was educated at Thomastown National School and De La Salle College, Waterford. He has spent his life engaged in productive agriculture, and on retirement has pursued his two great passions in life: travel and history. He is chairman of his local heritage society, and a contributor to its historical publication, *The Shadow of the Steeple*. Michael has travelled widely, to places as far apart as Australia, South America, Canada, Asia and Europe. *Freney the Robber* is his first historical work, and is intended as a candid look at life in the suppressed Ireland of the eighteenth century, when Freney and his kind were forced into a life of crime. To collect and record the folklore of Freney – Kilkenny's most notorious highwayman – has been his long-cherished ambition.